From Colin Kaepernick to Donald Trump: A New Age of Crisis

Dwayne Wong (Omowale)

DEDICATION

To my friends, family, and those fighting to make the world a better place.

CONTENTS

1 INTRODUCTION

The first version of *The Black African Crisis in the Age of a Black President* was written in July of 2014. The overall message of that short book was that African people face a global crisis and that the presidency of Barack Obama, although much celebrated, had failed to truly resolve that crisis. The book is told through a series of interviews, short speeches, and essays that involve a fictional character named Eddie Wilson. Eddie Wilson is skeptical that Obama's presidency will dramatically improve the condition of African people. Throughout the book, Wilson maintains the view that Obama's presidency is severely limited when it comes to addressing the plight of African people and that Obama's election does not necessarily represent progress. This book was meant to be a reflection of my own skeptical feelings about Obama throughout his two terms. My position was one of skepticism because I did not want to rush to formulate any judgments about Obama as a leader before he finished his two terms, but by 2014 I also felt that it was very apparent that even though a black man was finally president of America, the global crisis that African people experienced persisted. As I noted, that book was originally written in 2014. It has undergone a number of revisions since then.

The political situation which the first book was set in was much different than the one that produced this book. The first book covers a period from 2008 when Obama was nominated as the presidential candidate for the Democratic Party until 2014. The time period in which *The Black African Crisis in the Age of a*

1

Black President covers is around when the Black Lives Matter movement was now beginning to form. It had not yet become an international movement. At the time Colin Kaepernick had not created a national controversy by refusing to stand for the national anthem. There was not much of a national movement against racism and police brutality that was comparable to the movements that have emerged since then. In fact, one of the topics discussed in the first book is the fact that the civil rights movement in the 1960s had regressed to the point that there was no national movement fighting for real change.

It was especially noteworthy to me to see the emergence of Black Lives Matter and Kaepernick kneeling during Obama's presidency. It seemed to have confirmed the skepticism and criticism expressed in the first book by demonstrating that although Obama was president, the struggles of African Americans continued; the crisis that African people face continued.

The first book evolved from the interview between John Walks and Eddie Wilson that is found in the third chapter of that book. I decided to write a back and forth discussion on Pan-Africanism and reverse racism because I felt that the best way to address this topic was to lay it out in a debate format so that readers could see both sides of the issue. I ended up doing an entire book on exchanges which involved the fictional character of Eddie Wilson. Eddie Wilson is the name of the main character in a movie screenplay that I had been working on when I was in middle school.

When I wrote the first book, I envisioned Eddie Wilson as an extension of myself in many respects, although Wilson is presented as someone who is older and more experienced in the Pan-African struggle than I was at the time that these discussions were taking place. Eddie Wilson was meant to be a representation of some of my own views, but as a fictional character Eddie Wilson allowed me to participate in conversations and debates that I was not able to actually participate in. One example is the discussion that Eddie Wilson is involved in after Obama wins the nomination for the Democratic Party. At the time I was seventeen and I certainly did not have the knowledge to engage in a political conversation like the one that Eddie Wilson is involved in, but the character of Eddie Wilson allowed me to travel through time and discuss the reality that electing black faces to positions of power has never liberated African people. Of course, I was also writing with the benefit of hindsight as well.

That exchange also includes two other fictional characters who also present different perspectives to the topic as well. This is another area where using the character of Eddie Wilson is useful because it allows the reader to see an exchange of differing and sometimes conflicting ideas. This book also contains some back and forth exchanges as well. Writing from the perspective of those who disagree with Eddie Wilson was a challenge because it forced me to view the world from outside of my own perspectives. For this reason, the thought process behind writing these books is certainly much different than most of the other books that I have written, but that process being that writing these books has also allowed me to broaden some of my own views. I firmly believe that one cannot never truly understand one's own position until one also understands the opposing position.

For this book, I decided to bring Eddie Wilson back to discuss Donald Trump's presidency. As I said, the political situation at the time that I wrote *The Black African Crisis in the Age of a Black President* was much different than the situation at the time of writing this second book. This book is less concerned with addressing any illusions that some of us may have had about Obama's presidency being a period of progression for African people. The central focus of this second book is the conditions and circumstances that led to both Colin Kaepernick's protests and Donald Trump being elected president, although I do address a number of other topics as well.

The failures of Obama's presidency in a sense led to the conditions which caused both Kaepernick's protests against racial injustice and Trump's presidential campaign, so in that regard I consider this book to be a continuation of the theme of the previous book. The crisis that I discussed in the previous book was the crisis that African people faced in the age of a black president; the crisis that confronted us during Obama's presidency. The "new crisis" which I write about in this book is the crisis that African people are now faced with under the Trump administration.

2 A RESPONSE TO PRIME MINISTER CAMERON

This is a short response to statements that Britain's Prime Minister David Cameron made in Jamaica regarding reparations in 2015. Prime Minister Cameron suggested that Jamaicans need to move on from slavery, so Eddie Wilson decided to respond by demonstrating that Britain benefitted greatly from the enslavement and colonization of African people in the Caribbean.

In September 2015, Prime Minister David Cameron spoke in Jamaica where he urged Britain and Jamaica to "move on from this painful legacy and continue to build for the future". This comment was made after various Caribbean countries, including Jamaica, demanded that reparations be paid for slavery. The implications of Prime Minister Cameron's comments were very clear; he had no intention of offering reparations to Caribbean nations which have been adversely impacted by slavery.

    This is hardly surprising. Western nations have benefitted a great deal from slavery, but since slavery has been abolished those nations were content on maintaining the economic imbalance and inequality that slavery produced. Cameron seems of the legacy of slavery as if it is some immaterial legacy, but the reality is that slavery produced real tangible advancements for Western civilization. The legacy of slavery is not something that we can move on from because it is a legacy of exploitation that is still with us today. The Codrington Library in Oxford was paid for by slave labor—Christopher Codrington was a slave owner in Barbados. The legacy of slavery does not go away simply because David Cameron wishes that it goes away. We still see the underdevelopment of African people as a result of five-hundred years of oppression by Europeans. And, as I pointed out, this oppression allowed Europe to build institutions such as the Codrington Library.

When the European powers began colonizing the Caribbean islands, they wiped out the existing population. Bartolome de las Casas described Jamaica as being "unpeopled and desolate." Casas documented the destructive impact that European settlement had in the Caribbean, but, as David Walker pointed out, it was de las Casas who "proposed to his countrymen, the Spaniards in Hispaniola, to import the Africans from the Portuguese settlement in Africa, to dig up gold and silver, and work their plantations for them, to effect which, he made a voyage thence to Spain, and opened the subject to his master, Ferdinand, then in declining health, who listened to the plan; but who died soon after, and left it in the hands of his successor, Charles V." The massacre of the native people directly laid the foundation for the slave trade.

The slave trade was a lucrative business for Europe. The Church was involved in this. In *Capitalism and Slavery*, Eric Williams writes about a church elder who would thank God that "another cargo of benighted beings had been brought to a land where they could have the benefit of a gospel dispensation." Religious institutions played an important role in justifying the slave trade, but the planters were more concerned about profit than religion. Planters opposed introducing their slaves to Christianity and planters refused to give their slaves Sundays off. Even some Quakers were involved in the slave trade as well. Just about every segment of European society was involved in the slave trade and profited from that trade, so we are discussing the very economic development of Europe and the underdevelopment of Africa.

There should be no mistakes made about why the slave trade persisted as long as it did. In 1783, Prime Minister Lord North in England considered it an impossibility to abolish the slave trade because of how profitable it was for Europe. The claim for reparations is rooted in the understanding that slavery enriched Europeans, while also impoverishing African people. This is an imbalance which continues to this day. This process of underdevelopment simply did not end when slavery ended.

To demonstrate the underdevelopment which occurred during colonialism I will start by using Dominica as an example of the kind of conflicts that happened following the end of slavery. In 1838, Dominica had a black majority in the Dominican House of Assembly. The legislators in Dominica began advocating that voting rights be granted to freed people without property—at the time those who did not own property could not vote, and therefore the system was set up to the advantage of the wealthy property-owning white folks. The British on the island organized a political party of their own and took back control from the black people of the island. This was the type of conflict that we saw all throughout the British West Indies. The former slaves were engaged in a struggle to obtain greater political freedom and economic security. Slavery was over, but the newly freed Africans still found themselves working for the former slave masters and making a pittance for their labor.

This happened too in Guyana. Following the end of slavery many Africans preferred to work for themselves than work for the former slave masters, so laws were implemented to restrict this freedom to make the African population more dependent on the Europeans. The European planters also started importing cheap labor from other parts of the world as well, which further restricted the power of the African population since this importer labor replaced the labor of African people.

The European system of exploitation is one that was quite universal. Both the Dutch and the British controlled Guyana, and they ruled in the same manner. The Dutch first settled Guyana in 1616. There was a war between the Netherlands and Britain in 1781. The result of this war was that the British occupied Guyana for a few months. The Dutch were able to retake Guyana in 1784, but the British would return again in 1796 when they launched an invasion of the Dutch colonies by sending troops from Barbados. The British controlled Guyana from 1796 until 1802 before returning Guyana to the Dutch once more. The Dutch ruled Demerara and Essequibo as separate colonies, but both colonies were ceded to Britain formally in 1814. By 1831 both colonies were unified as British Guiana and it would remain a British colony until independence. This type of situation is not unique. Trinidad passed from Spain to England. St. Lucia, Dominica, and Grenada were French colonies that were taken over by the British.

What is worth noting is that although Guyana passed between the Dutch and the English, the system of oppression that existed remained the same. Both were colonial European oppressors who maintained a planter dominated society in which Europeans were at the top of the social structure, and Africans were slave labor. The British and the Dutch may have fought each other over control of Guyana, but they both agreed on the premise that Europeans were superior and should dominate African people.

This system of racist exploitation was so entrenched in Guyana that Walter Rodney explained: "During the slave era, candidates for membership of the Court of Policy were required to own no fewer than twenty-five slaves. Subsequently, the qualification became ownership of no less than eight acres of land, at least half of which had to be under cultivation."

In other words, owning slaves was at one point a qualification for membership in the Court of Policy. And we know that because one had to be a slave owner to qualify for membership, the type of laws that were being passed were obviously laws that were in favor of the slave owners. When slavery ended, there were still wealth qualifications for membership. Among the type of policies that were passed by Guyana's legislature were taxes that were placed on former slaves.

African people put up resistance against the oppression of slavery. This fact is well-known. In Guyana, for example, there was a revolt led by an enslaved African man known as Kofi or Cuffy. James Rodway described Cuffy's rebellion as "probably the most disastrous slave revolt that ever occurred in any colony." Rodway notes smaller acts of rebellion as well, such as a slave master who moved to Guyana from Barbados who was murdered in 1774 by two of his slaves. This resistance against oppression continued even after slavery was abolished, but rather than violent uprisings these rebellions took the form of organized labour movements.

Around the 1920s and 1930s, we begin to see labor movements being organized throughout the British West Indies. These labor movements served as the forerunner for political independence. In

1940, the Antigua Trades and Labour Union was created. From this labor union came the Antiguan Labour Party. Vere Bird was among the candidates that were elected from this party. Vere Bird became Antigua and Barbuda's first prime minister when the country gained its independence in 1981. By 1951 the efforts of the Antigua Trades and Labour Union had helped to secure complete adult suffrage.

In St. Kitts and Nevis, the Workers League was organized by Robert Bradshaw in 1932. By 1940 the organization was renamed the St. Kitts and Nevis Trades and Labour Union. This union also established a political wing known as the St. Kitts and Nevis Labour Party. Bradshaw was elected into the Legislative Council in 1946. Bradshaw would go on to serve as the first premier of St. Kitts and Nevis. The St. Kitts and Nevis Labour Party eventually fell out of favor with the people because of its tendency towards repression and dominance, which would become a common theme among Caribbean political parties.

There was a struggle for freedom in St. Vincent as well. In St. Vincent, Ebenezer Joshua and Milton Cato emerged as two important political leaders who challenged British colonialism in St. Vincent, although they challenged each other as well. Joshua agitated against the colonial masters, the plantation owners, and the business class, who were all exploiters of the Vincentian people. Joshua denounced both Cato and the British government, stating: "We must from the very out start attack the British Government for its open complicity in abandoning people whom they have used for centuries to develop a vast colonial empire. Now they trade us off to the wolves and have secured their Mafia types agents to seek our blood in their take over, the State of Saint Vincent was now run by an errant dictatorship which was seeking openly to fight the unarmed people of Saint Vincent."

Joshua accused Cato of using British agents to broadcast false information exclusively controlled by a dictatorship, giving false information about the acts of the government. Cato similarly criticized Joshua and British colonialism. In the end, Cato emerged victorious in the political struggle. Cato and his Saint Vincent Labour Party led the nation into independence in 1979. I mention the rivalry between the two men to note that the political rivalry between the two was also framed in terms of opposition to British colonialism as well. Though the two men were rivals, they were both critical of colonial rule in St. Vincent

The colonial government was so negligent towards the people of their colonies that in the 1930s there was widespread protest against the poor economic state that people were living in. The British responded by dispatching a Royal Commission that was led by Lord Moyne, which is why it became known as the Moyne Commission. This commission visited the region and reported on the poor conditions in the British West Indies.

References:

Alwyn Westfield, "The Impact of Leadership on Politics and Political Development in St. Vincent and the Grenadines Under Ebenezer Theodore Joshua and Robert Milton Cato," (dissertation), 2012.

Bartolomé de las Casas, *A Brief Account of the Destruction of the Indies*

David Walker, *Walker's Appeal*, 1830.

Eric Williams, *Capitalism and Slavery*, 1944.

James Rodway, *History of British Guiana*, 1891.

Rowena Mason, "Jamaica should 'move on from painful legacy of slavery', says Cameron," *The Guardian,* September 30, 2015.

Sandra W. Meditz and Dennis M. Hanratty (editors), *Islands of the Commonwealth Caribbean: A Regional Study*. Washington: GPO for the Library of Congress, 1989.

Walter Rodney, *A History of the Guyanese Working People, 1881-1905*, (Johns Hopkins University Press, 1981).

3 THE DEMOCRATIC ESTABLISHMENT HAS FAILED

This is an article written by Eddie Wilson following Donald Trump's inauguration. In this article, Wilson details some of the missteps and mistakes that the Democrats made, which resulted in Donald Trump being elected. Eddie Wilson is especially critical of the mistakes which were made during Obama's presidency.

Last week we witnessed the inauguration of the new president of the United States, Donald Trump. Trump's surprise victory over Hillary Clinton last year has raised many questions not only about the future of the Democratic Party, but also about the two terms that Barack Obama served as president as well. One would think that after eight years of profound social and economic change, the American masses would have eagerly filed in line to vote for yet another Democratic president, but this was not the case because there was no eight years of profound change. There were eight years of struggle and, for those of us who had high hopes in Obama's presidency, eight years of disappointments, with a few victories.

To be clear, Clinton lost because of the electoral college, but the Obama coalition fell apart at a time when Obama and the Democratic Party needed them the most. It fell apart because of how fragile it was from the onset. Obama swept into power in

2008 offering hope and optimistic rhetoric, but eight years later not enough had changed. Clinton won enough votes to win the popular vote, but she lost in the states where it really counted, and she lost in some important states that Obama had won.

When Obama was first nominated as the presidential candidate for the Democratic Party—defeating Hillary Clinton in the process—I wrote a piece called "The Black African Crisis in the Age of a Black President." The point that I wished to convey was that the mere election of a black man as president of the United States was not in of itself a sign of true progress for African Americans. I pointed out that in other parts of the world we saw black faces come into positions of political power, yet the same inequality and oppression continued. I mentioned the struggles in South Africa after Nelson Mandela's historic presidency and the struggles in Trinidad under Eric Williams. My position at the time was one of skepticism because I did not believe that if Obama was elected—and at the time it seemed more likely than not that he would be elected—the situation of African Americans and African people around the world would change very much. I was right.

The Obama administration continued an imperialistic foreign policy in Africa, which can be demonstrated by Obama's support for Paul Kagame. Kagame has earned the praise of Tony Blair and Bill Clinton. He has spoken at Harvard and earned honorary doctorates from Western universities. All of these Western leaders and institutions ignored the human rights situation in Rwanda. Critics of Kagame have been killed, imprisoned, or driven into exile.

Obama's government was Kagame's closest ally. As *Politico*'s report points out, Kagame was trained in the United States before returning to Rwanda to seize power in 1994. The United States has provided Kagame with both military aid and diplomatic cover for his abuses. The United Nations has documented how Kagame has committed numerous human rights violations, including the massacre of tens of thousands of civilians. Susan Rice, who served as Obama's Secretary of State, reportedly stated that the only thing that America has to do is "look the other way." As American ambassador to the United Nations, Rice apparently tried to get the rest of the world to look the other way by attempting to block the publication of a 2010 U.N. report about these killings.

The United States finally suspended some of its military aid to Kagame after evidence from the U.N. demonstrated that Rwanda was supporting rebel groups in the Democratic Republic of the Congo, but millions of dollars in foreign aid continued and the government was openly considering reinstating the suspended funds. Kagame is certainly not the only dictator that Obama supported, but Kagame is the one which I focus on here because of how close his relationship has been to the United States and because of the praise and accolades that he has received from Western institutions. The United States was giving millions of dollars in aid to a government which was committing war crimes in another African country and then the United States attempted to cover up those crimes.

This was the legacy of Obama and Rice in Africa. That's right. Two people of African descent were engaged in an imperialistic foreign policy in Africa. I mention this because one of the legacies that Obama left behind is one of disillusionment among many African Americans who were hopeful about change and hopeful about transformation. Instead, under Obama's presidency we saw the emergence of the Black Lives Matter movement in response to all of the killings of unarmed African Americans. Under Obama's presidency we witnessed protests in Ferguson and Baltimore in response to the police killings of black people. The issue of police killing black people caused Colin Kaepernick to decide that he was going to kneel for the national anthem during football games. African Americans were angry and demanding change, which they had not seen under Obama's leadership.

African people were facing a global crisis before Obama came into power. After eight years of being president, Obama failed to properly address our plight, but the issue was much larger than a failure to address the plight of African Americans. Under Obama, the United States witnessed record numbers of poverty, yet there did not appear to be any urgency in addressing this issue on the part of the administration. During Obama's first term, he did not even seem to want to directly address the issue of poverty.

The appeal of Bernie Sanders, and to some extent Trump as well, was that these candidates spoke to the fears and frustrations of voters. They also offered something different than the typical type of politicians which the American public had grown tired of.

There was a clear repudiation of the establishment within both major political parties. We also saw some level of repudiation of the two-party system itself. In 2016, Jill Stein of the Green Party was able to garner a bit more interest than in the prior election.

Some Democrats saw Sanders and Stein as clear problems for Clinton's election, with some polls suggesting that only 55 percent of Sanders supporters were supportive of Clinton. There was talk that these dissatisfied Sanders voters would make an exodus out of the Democratic Party and towards the Green Party. The Democratic Party simply was not progressive enough for some voters and the Green Party seemed like a viable option.

Democrats were concerned that Stein would split the votes, allowing Trump to win the election. The fact is that this is what Stein herself intended to do. When David Cobb ran in 2004, he pursued a "safe state" strategy of only targeting voters in predominantly Democratic states, but Stein was not interested in such a strategy. In 2000, Ralph Nader was accused of contributing to Al Gore's defeat in Florida and was labeled as a "spoiler" in that election. Stein had no fear of being labeled as a spoiler. The Green Party was clearly trying to attract frustrated Democrats who were tired of being told to vote for the lesser of two evils when there were other options outside of the Democrats and Republicans. When looking for reasons to explain why Clinton lost to Trump, some will inevitably look to blame the Green Party.

One could make the case that had every single person who voted for Jill Stein voted for Hillary Clinton instead, then Clinton would have won. Democrats said the same thing in 2000 when they blamed Ralph Nader for spoiling the election and helping George W. Bush to win the election. So, if you think that only the Democrats and Republicans have the right to run candidates for political office, then the Green Party and other parties are spoilers. My position is different from that view.

Let us say, for the sake of argument, that Nader was responsible for the Democrats losing to Bush in 2000. If that was the case, then the Democrats should have respected the fact that the Green Party is a party with a significant national following. Hillary Clinton should have been working to win over some of the Jill Stein voters, but instead the only thing that the Democratic Party did was warn the American people against voting for a third party. Remember when Michelle Obama said that a protest vote would help Trump? Some Democrats were upset with their party and voted for Jill Stein as a protest vote, but the Green Party is also a political party that has been around for some time and has a following. There are people who are registered members of the Green Party, and they vote for the Green Party in every election. These individuals were not engaging in a protest vote. They were merely voting for their political party.

Now, did Jill Stein spoil the elections in 2012 when Obama won? In 2012, no one in the Democratic Party was even concerned about Jill Stein, but Stein became a cause for concern in 2016 because a lot of people were so disillusioned with the Democratic Party that a larger number of people were supporting the Green Party. Many of these people were people that were supporting Bernie Sanders and realized that if they could not vote for Bernie in the general election, then they could vote for a political candidate that shares some of Bernie's socialist views.

The Democrats engaged in an incorrect strategy in addressing the potential issue of the Green Party. First Lady Michelle Obama explained in a campaign speech for Hillary Clinton: "Here's the truth: either Hillary Clinton or her opponent will be elected president this year. And if you vote for someone other than Hillary, or if you don't vote at all, then you are helping to elect Hillary's opponent." Barack Obama expressed the same views when he stated that "if you vote for a third-party candidate who's got no chance to win, that's a vote for Trump." Rather than offering a reason for why Green Party supporters should vote for the Democrats, the tactic was merely to scare voters into supporting Clinton because not doing so would allow Trump to win.

If you are a serious politician, then you have to know how to play the political game and playing that game means that you have to study the field of play. If you know that in 2016 you will have to run against the Republican Party and the Green Party, and whatever other party is on the ballot, then you prepare to campaign against all of your opponents. You have to put together a coalition to win. Obama did it twice in 2008 and 2012, so the claim that Jill Stein spoiled the election comes across to me as an excuse for the fact that Hillary Clinton was an unpopular and disliked candidate who failed to bring together the Democratic Party after a contentious primary between herself and Bernie Sanders.

If anything, Clinton's actions in the primary helped to further divide the party. Representative Debbie Wasserman Schultz was forced to step down as the chair of the Democratic National Convention (DNC) when leaked emails revealed that she favored Hillary Clinton's campaign over Bernie Sanders. This exposed that the Democratic establishment had a bias against Sanders. Everyone knew this, but the leak confirmed it. Donna Brazile took over as the interim chair. There was yet another scandal when it was leaked that Brazile sent information regarding one of the questions for an upcoming town hall to Clinton's campaign. These leaks exposed how corrupt and dishonest the DNC was, and Clinton did not speak out against any of this because she was benefitting from these unfair actions. That these scandals were revealed through leaks made the situation even worse. What else has been going on behind the scenes that no one knew about? What other corruption was there that had not yet been exposed?

The loss to Trump was also a political miscalculation by the Democrats and by those who support the Democratic Party. In 2012, those of us who were critical of the Democratic Party were told to vote for Obama because he was the lesser of the two evils. Even those who understood that Obama had not done enough to address the challenges that African Americans faced saw Obama as a better alternative to what the Republican Party was offering. This same logic was used again in 2016. There were those who were aware of Hillary Clinton's many faults, but the lesser of two evils logic was once again used to provide a reasoning for why those of us who had serious criticisms of Hillary Clinton should vote for her anyway.

I understand it. For many, Trump's rhetoric was simply too racist, misogynistic, and frankly repugnant for anyone to seriously consider him as a legitimate choice for the presidency. No matter how bad Hillary Clinton is, Trump presented something much worse. Jill Stein may have been an alternative, but not a practical one. Stein was not going to win in 2016 and I am sure even she was aware of this. Had she followed Bernie Sanders' example and attempted to run in the Democratic Party, she might have built up a larger national platform for herself and her ideas, but she did not do so. The only two real options were Clinton and Trump, and for most Americans it was simply a matter of choosing the lesser of the two evils. I am not inclined to blame anyone who voted for Clinton or who voted for Stein. This political system is one which deliberately restricts the options of the American citizenry and those who choose to participate in the electoral system understand this. It is also a system that is built on fear. People who vote for the lesser of the two evils do so not necessarily because they support the candidate which they are voting for, but because they fear that the other candidate may be elected to office.

I put the blame on the Democratic establishment for its failures to truly transform America in the eight years that Obama was president. I understand that because of the separation of powers in the American political system that there were certain things that Obama could not accomplish without a Democratic majority in Congress, but more could have been done still. As we saw in Baltimore and Ferguson, Obama could have easily utilized the Department of Justice to address racism in the police force. Obama could have scaled back American imperialism, especially in Africa. Obama did not need a Democratic majority to withdraw support from the likes of Kagame in Rwanda and other dictators in Africa. Obama could have also been more vocal about addressing the root of wealth inequality in America. There were things that should have been done that were not done.

Despite the criticisms to be made of Democratic Party, we were told that in 2016 we should vote for Clinton because, at the very least, she is a better option than Trump. This was the same argument that was made in 2012 when many of us who were skeptical of Obama were expressing our criticisms of some of his policies. Trump's victory exposed the weaknesses and the failure of the Democratic Party. The party has so allowed itself to think of itself as the party of progress that it failed to truly understand and connect with the suffering and the frustration of the average American citizen. Perhaps most importantly, Trump's election exposed the shallowness of the approach of trying to scare voters into voting for the perceived lesser of two evils. It creates the type of voter disappointment and apathy which allows for candidates like Donald Trump to be elected.

Bibliography:

Anjan Sindaram, "Rwanda: The Darling Dictator," *Politico*, Mar/Apr. 2014.

Bill Scher, "'Think You've Got it Locked Hillary'" Meet Jill Stein," *Politico*, June 19, 2016.

Hadas Gold, "Brazile denies giving Clinton camp advance notice on CNN town hall question, *Politico*, October 11, 2016.

Jennifer Epstein, "Obama on poverty: Few mentions," *Politico*, September 16, 2012.

Louis Nelson, "Michelle Obama pitches Clinton: 'It's not about voting for the perfect candidate'" *Politico*, September 28, 2016.

A Reply from Ryan Dinkins

Good evening, Eddie,

I recently read your piece on the Democratic establishment and I am not sure that I would agree with your conclusion. I think what happened was a terrible outcome for our country and that the election was stolen from Hillary Clinton. The truth will come out one day soon and I think it will indicate that Russia played a very big role in influencing this election in favor of Trump.

I also think you were too defensive of Jill Stein. Not only did Russia cost us this election, but so too did the Greens. Jill Stein had no hope of winning this election and she should have just supported the Democrats to beat Trump. Instead, we received the worst possible outcome for this election. We have a madman as president and I am greatly concerned for the future of our nation. I understand that you disliked President Obama, but Trump will offer us something much worse. I hope you see that.

Eddie Wilson responds:

I understand those concerns, but I think if Democrats ran a better campaign they would have won. I don't think Russia forced people to sit out this election. That happened because people did not like the two options which were put in front of them. As for the Green Party, I did not support the Green Party. If anything, I've been just as critical of them for their failures. Donald Trump was able to hijack the Republican Party and win by playing a populist. Bernie Sanders, who I think may be a bit more sincere than Trump, came close to doing the same thing for the Democrats. I think if the Green Party was serious, they should have truly embraced the "spoiler" label by having Jill Stein run for the Democrats, to disrupt the party the same way that Trump did for the Republicans. At the very least, it would have helped the Green Party secure more national attention and more votes.

Where Trump is concerned, I will continue struggling for what it is that I have been struggling for regardless of who is in the White House; whether it be a Republican, a Democrat or even a Green. I do not think any of them serve the interests of African people. They were all parties which are primarily focused on the white majority in America, including the Green Party. I do not dislike Jill Stein. I think she was one of the more sincere candidates, but I do not think that the Green Party is radical enough to truly disrupt the two-party system, and by disrupt I am not referring to winning elections. I am referring to making both of the parties in power nervous. I think they were nervous in 2016 because of how unpopular Trump and Clinton were, but I would like to see a third party which is really interested in shaking things up like Trump did. The Communist Party was a party like that, but the Green Party is not, unfortunately.

There needs to be more of an effort to make the Green Party a viable option. Cornel West's endorsement of the Green Party was helpful, but West only did so after Bernie Sanders failed to win the nomination. Sanders endorsed Hillary Clinton, but West could not. West did not come out in support of Stein in 2012. If he had done so, perhaps the Greens would have been in a better position to win, but as far as I am concerned, voting for Jill Stein in 2016 was a waste of a vote because she had no chance to win. That is my view on the issue.

4 COLIN KAEPERNICK'S PROTEST

This is a paper that was written by Eddie Wilson about Colin Kaepernick's protest. This chapter also includes a reply to the paper and Eddie Wilson's response to that reply.

When asked why he was refusing to stand for the national anthem, Colin Kaepernick declared: "I am not going to stand up to show pride in a flag for a country that oppresses black people and people of color." What is profound to me is that Kaepernick was making this statement at the time when a black man was the president of the country. That statement expressed the neglect and frustration that black people continued to feel eight years after the election of the nation's first black president.

Kaepernick continued on to discuss his disillusionment with both Hillary Clinton and Donald Trump, both of whom ran for the presidency last year. Kaepernick stated that "you have Hillary who's called black teens or black kids super predators. You have Donald Trump who's openly racist." I find this especially interesting because Kaepernick was expressing the same view that Malcolm X expressed when he stated: "I'm not a Republican, nor a Democrat, nor an American, and got sense enough to know it." He would continue on in that speech to describe himself as a victim of Americanism. African Americans today are still victims of Americanism, which is why Kaepernick felt that it was necessary to kneel for the national anthem.

President Obama's remarks on the situation were rather

interesting to me as well. Last year, Obama stated: "I think there are a lot of ways you can do it. As a general matter, when it comes to the flag and the national anthem and the meaning that that holds for our men and women in uniform and those who fought for us, that is a tough thing for them to get past to then hear what his deeper concerns are." Notice that Obama mentions what the flag means for the men and women who have served America militarily.

When Kaepernick was kneeling, he was in fact kneeling on behalf of men and women who have worn America's uniform. He was kneeling for people like Kenneth Chamberlain Sr., a former Marine who was shot and killed by police officers in his own home in 2011 when his medical alert pendant went off and the police were called to provide medical assistance for him. Chamberlain wore the uniform and what did that get him? Chamberlain was called a nigger by one of the officers before they forced their way into his apartment after Chamberlain refused to allow the officers in. What did the flag and the national anthem mean for Chamberlain? Did it protect him against police violence?

I also want to make a point here about how American society perceives black athletes because this is a point that is relevant to how I view Kaepernick's protests. There was a report from the *New York Post* that I will quote here: "The Minnesota Vikings running back had at least five children out of wedlock and could have had as many as seven, according to one of his ex-girlfriends." The story notes that one of these children, a two-year old who was killed after being beaten, was not seen by Peterson until that child was in a coma. So, we have black men who father many children that they are not raising, yet the outrage is against Kaepernick merely because Kaepernick decided to speak out against an injustice. Why?

The answer to this is that American society does not like when a black man takes the type of stance against injustice that Kaepernick did. It is fine for a black man to be like Peterson by fathering children that he is not raising. In fact, that merely confirms certain racial stereotypes about black men, but it goes against the stereotype for a black man to do what Kaepernick did. To understand this, I want to assess Joe Louis, who is in some ways the prototype for the safe and apolitical black athlete.

Joe Louis's son explained: "What my father did was enable white America to think of him as an American, not as a black." One of the ways that Louis achieved this was by maintaining a very politically and racially neutral image. This caused some to denounce Louis as an Uncle Tom, which is an assessment that may not be entirely fair to Louis. Larry Schwartz explained: "While some accused Louis of being an Uncle Tom, others realized it wasn't in his training or character to be militant. His uncommon sense of dignity, exemplified by his refusal to be pictured with a slice of watermelon, increased his popularity." Louis was certainly a much different public figure than the previous black heavyweight champion, Jack Johnson. Johnson was especially infamous for his love of white women, which got him into legal trouble when he was convicted for transporting a white woman across state lines.

Louis would not degrade himself in public, yet he also did not take any significant public stance against racism either—at least, not an uncompromisingly critical stance against racism. This is why white people felt comfortable with Louis. White Americans also saw Louis as an American hero after he defeated the German boxer Max Schmeling in their rematch—Louis had previously lost to Schmeling. For Americans, Louis' victory was a victory against the Nazi regime. The fight meant so much to the country that Louis was invited to the White House where he met President Franklin Roosevelt.

Louis did more than merely beat a German boxer in the ring, however. Louis eagerly supported America's cause in World War II. This included donating his money to military relief funds and enlisting in the army to support the war effort. He went so far as to say that America would win the war because "we're on God's side." America went into the war with a segregated army, but this was the nation which Louis was proclaiming was on God's side. I am not suggesting that Louis should have sided with or praised the Nazis, but that statement certainly conveys Louis' uncritical praise for America. But this is precisely what made him a hero to some. Louis was safe. He would never challenge the status quo.

Life for Louis outside of the boxing ring was much less heroic. Like many athletes, Louis was a prolific womanizer. Among those that Louis had affairs with included Lena Horne. This caused a strain in Louis' marital life. He was married four times, including marrying his first wife a second time. Louis' extravagances and his generosity with money caused him a lot of issues with money. He ended up owing over one million dollars in back taxes, interest, and penalties. Louis turned to pro-wrestling to help pay off his debts. He eventually became addicted to cocaine as well.

I mention this not to denigrate Louis, but to point out that in a system of racial oppression and domination, African men must be more than mere athletes. We must take principled stands because the money and the women that so many athletes seem to enjoy when they think that they have arrived within the system is fleeting, but one's integrity is not. Louis may have been a champion in the ring, but his life should serve as a cautionary tale about the trappings of success for athletes who believe that their athletic prowess offers them any sort of real freedom or advancement within the system that continues to oppress African people around the world.

Louis obtained what so many of us long for. He had money; he had women; he had fame; and he had the respect of white America at a time when few black men did. What did any of this mean to him, however? Louis was not particularly good at managing his money, so it became a source of problems for him. One cannot eat fame or spend it, so Louis' status as a world class boxer meant little once he no longer had money. As I have stated before, Louis was divorced several times. Is having an abundance of women more meaningful than maintaining a stable family life? Finally, did Louis ever truly have the respect of white America? Was he respected as a man or was he merely respected as a boxer who was too safe and too uncontroversial to truly speak out against racial oppression?

Louis would not allow himself to be reduced to demeaning stereotypes, but he was also careful to craft an image that was safe to white audiences. Though Louis would have affairs with white women, Louis never allowed himself to be photographed with a white woman in public. He also never gloated over defeated opponents or engaged in fixed fights. He presented a carefully crafted clean image to the public, which was a bit different from who Louis was in his private life. I do not write this to demean Louis, but merely to point out the fact that he presented a particular image of himself to the white public, but that image was not helpful for Louis in his own personal life. This is what black people must understand. Conformity to white expectations is not always healthy for our own personal growth.

Given that he is biracial, Kaepernick could have decided to take a racially neutral position like Tiger Woods did. Woods described himself as "Cablinasian." He is a mix of Caucasian, black, and Asian. Woods admitted that it bothers him when people identify him as an African American because he does not identify himself as such.

Woods' position is not unique. Given the oppression that African people have endured, there is a negative connotation that comes with our identity, so there are those like Woods who opt to reject the African identity by invoking his multiracial make-up, knowing full well that he lives in a racist society which cares very little about making such distinctions.

More importantly is the fact that maintaining racial neutrality allows one to avoid taking a stand against racial injustice. It is, in some respects, a position of cowardice in the face of real suffering and real injustice. It is a position that says, "I am black, but I am not one of those blacks, so feel free to abuse 'those blacks', but respect the fact that I am different from them." Kaepernick could have taken this position, but he decided not to.

Woods is not the only athlete who has tried to be neutral on racial issues. When asked about the killing of Trayvon Martin, Kobe Bryant stated: "I won't react to something just because I'm supposed to, because I'm an African-American. That argument doesn't make any sense to me. So we want to advance as a society and as a culture, but, say, if something happens to an African-American, we immediately come to his defense? Yet you want to talk about how far we've progressed as a society? Well, if we've progressed as a society, then you don't jump to somebody's defense just because they're African-American." What was funny about this response was that Kobe was the one who made it about race when he didn't have to. Trayvon Martin could have been a different race and what happened to him would have been equally as wrong, but Kobe Bryant wanted to make himself appear racially neutral. In doing so, he made himself appear insensitive to the fact that Trayvon was a teenage boy who did not deserve to be killed. Then there was Michael Jordan who is quoted as having remarked that Republicans buy shoes too. He would not let activism hurt his brand or his shoe sales.

There are some who would suggest that Kaepernick is an ungrateful athlete who should just remain silent because he is rich and successful, and therefore has nothing to complain about regarding racial oppression in America. The implication is that a black person who attains a certain degree of success in America should just stay silent and not speak out against injustices. The logic behind this is that black people should concern ourselves with advancing to a point where racism does not directly impact us and once we have reached this point, we should just ignore the pain and suffering of others. This is the type of individualism and selfishness which we are expected to have in this system, but we must resist it. Harriet Tubman did not only free herself by running away from the plantation. She returned to free others.

What should be understood from Kaepernick's act of protest is that an African within a racist and oppressive system can only achieve his highest self through resistance, through striving for freedom from the unjust system. This is also a position which connects one to his fellow man. In the spirit of the African concept of "Ubuntu," this position says that we are interconnected and the struggle of my brother or my sister is my struggle as well.

This is a position which commands respect, but true respect. The respect given to one who makes a moral and principled stance. This was the stance that Kaepernick took. Though he has received backlash from many for taking the stance that he has taken, how many of those who criticize Kaepernick can truly say that they have taken any sort of stance—no matter how unpopular it may be—for something they believed in. How many of them have taken a stance against an injustice in society? Kaepernick is not a leader or an activist in the traditional sense. He is a football player who became conscious of the oppression of African people in this country and took a stand against that oppression. For this Kaepernick deserves respect because he has set an example for others to follow.

References:

Ben McGrath, "Whom Does Kobe Bryant Represent?" *The New*

Yorker, April 1, 2014.

Hanna Trudo, "Obama: Kaepernick 'exercising his constitutional right to make a statement,'" *Politico*, September 5, 2016.

Larry Schwartz, "'Brown Bomber' was a hero to all," ESPN.

Leonard Greene, "Adrian Peterson could have 7 kids: ex," *New York Post*, October 17, 2013.

Ryan Deveraux, "Family of retired marine shot dead by police demands prosecution," *The Guardian*, May 9, 2012.

"Tiger Woods describes himself as 'Cablinasian,'" *Associated Press*, April 22, 1997.

A Response from a Critic:

I am writing this response to express my disagreement with your article. I think that it is very disrespectful to our nation and to our troops that Kaepernick would kneel during the national anthem. I understand that we still have racial inequality in our nation, but that is not the proper way to express disenchantment with racism in America. This is the reason why Kaepernick has received so much backlash. I also find it disgusting that in this same piece praising Kaepernick's act of disrespect, you would choose to denigrate a great American like Joe Louis who, unlike Kaepernick, actually served this great nation!

Eddie Wilson's Reply:

Which African who stood up against racism has ever been accepted in the United States? Rosa Parks and Martin Luther King certainly were not. They were both jailed for their activism. And keep in mind that Martin Luther King was considered more acceptable to America than the Nation of Islam and the Black Panther Party were. Malcolm X pointed this out when he said in an interview that when the Nation of Islam expressed a desire not to mix with whites they called the Nation a hate group, but Martin Luther King was running around telling black people to love all kind of white people and they sic dogs on Martin Luther King.

Both the separatist philosophy of the Nation of Islam and the integrationist approach of Martin Luther King were unacceptable for America, and both Martin Luther King and Elijah Muhammad had been jailed for their approaches to the injustices that were being inflicted against African Americans.

America has never accepted any African American that has stood up against racism. Kaepernick being criticized and denounced as he has been is just a continuation of that legacy and it demonstrates that African people are chastised for having an opinion or a view of this country that differs from the mainstream. This is why I said that as a people we are better off not trying to conform to America's standards because this is a society that does not want us to think for ourselves and does not want us to feel real emotions. This society does not want us to feel the real pain, hurt, and anger that we should be feeling over racial oppression.

As for your comments about me denigrating an American hero, all I will say is that my message to African athletes is stand for something greater than money, fame, and women because when you retire those things go away. Do not end up like a Joe Louis or many of the other safe athletes who never caused any controversies and who never challenged the system. I am not sure why that should be controversial or offensive to anyone, unless you are the type of person who wants African Americans to remain in the helpless and oppressed state that we are in.

I also want to thank you for your outrage because it is people like you who helped to elevate Kaepernick. The documentary *The Hate That Hate Produced* was meant to present a negative image of the Nation of Islam to scare Americans, but it did the opposite. People who watched the documentary were intrigued and wanted to know more about this movement. They wanted to know more about Malcolm X. So white racists end up creating an even bigger problem for themselves by giving attention to those that they disagree with. The same is true with Kaepernick. I would have never known about him kneeling if the media did not go out of its way to make such a big deal about it.

5 A REVIEW OF STATE OF EMERGENCY

This is a short essay that was written as a review of Patrick Buchanan's book, State of Emergency. In this review Eddie Wilson seeks to expose the insecurity of Buchanan's position and demonstrate that the greatest threat to Western civilization is internal, not external. This review is also followed by replies from two critics.

President Donald Trump spoke in Poland recently. There he expressed the idea of Western civilization being under threat. President Trump said:

"We urge Russia to cease its destabilizing activities in Ukraine and elsewhere, and its support for hostile regimes—including Syria and Iran—and to instead join the community of responsible nations in our fight against common enemies and in defense of civilization itself.

Finally, on both sides of the Atlantic, our citizens are confronted by yet another danger—one firmly within our control. This danger is invisible to some but familiar to the Poles: the steady creep of government bureaucracy that drains the vitality and wealth of the people. The West became great not because of paperwork and regulations but because people were allowed to chase their dreams and pursue their destinies."

Trump also went on to say in this speech: "The fundamental question of our time is whether the West has the will to survive. Do we have the confidence in our values to defend them at any cost? Do we have enough respect for our citizens to protect our borders? Do we have the desire and the courage to preserve our civilization in the face of those who would subvert and destroy it?" This speech played on the idea of Western civilization being under a threat and needing to defend itself. An aspect of Western civilization's fragility is the ever present need to defend itself, whether it is militarily or morally.

With Trump's remarks as the backdrop, I want to undertake this review of Buchanan's book, *State of Emergency: The Third World Invasion and Conquest*, because of the fact that so many of the views which Trump expressed in his speech in Poland were ideas that were being put forward by Buchanan years prior. Not only did Buchanan write about the need to protect America's borders, but Buchanan also wrote about this threat that Western civilization was facing and the need to defend the West from this threat.

The title of the book is meant to cause alarm and panic at this supposed Third World invasion. The concept of Third World is a very vaguely defined concept. It is most often used to describe poor and developing nations, but what the concept originally referred to were nations that were non-aligned in the Cold War. First World countries were the ones on the side of capitalist America and Second World countries were sided with the Soviet Union. I point this out because Buchanan himself never really defines what he means when he says Third World, although the implication he gives in this text is that he is referring to non-white people.

I think reviewing this book is also important because it demonstrates that Trump's ideas were not new. For some, Trump appears to be a sort of anomaly in politics, but I would make the case that Trump's ideas are actually deeply rooted in Western political tradition. It is for this reason that I do not try to link Trump's campaign to fascism or Nazism because elements of that type of thinking existed in America long before Adolf Hitler thought about them, so I do not believe that we have to necessarily look to Hitler to find the roots of Trump's political thought.

As far as African people are concerned the entire Western system is a fascist one. We were oppressed by the Germans, the Italians, and the Spanish, as well as the Americans, the British, and the French. I want to make this point very clear; the American system has always been a very racist and oppressive one since its founding, so I do not look to Nazi Germany to find the roots of Trump's political ideas. I look right here at America's history.

In *How Europe Underdeveloped Africa*, Walter Rodney argued that the Holocaust was merely a case of Western society's unchecked racism turning inwardly on itself. Rodney explained:

"In the short run, European racism seemed to have done Europeans no harm, and they used those erroneous ideas to justify their further domination of non-European peoples in the colonial epoch. But the international proliferation of bigoted and unscientific racist ideas was bound to have its negative consequences in the long run. When Europeans put millions of their brothers (Jews) into ovens under the Nazis, the chickens were coming home to roost. Such behaviour inside of 'democratic' Europe was not as strange as it is sometimes made out to be. There was always a contradiction between the elaboration of democratic ideas inside Europe and the elaboration of authoritarian and thuggish practices by Europeans with respect to Africans. When the French Revolution was made in the name of 'Liberty, Equality and Fraternity,' it did not extend to black Africans who were enslaved by France in the West Indies and the Indian Ocean. Indeed, France fought against the efforts of those people to emancipate themselves, and the leaders of their bourgeois revolution said plainly that they did not make it on behalf of black humanity."

The reality is that the message of the Nazis was nothing new. That element of racial superiority has existed in Western thought for a very long time. I don't want readers to be under the impression that we are seeing a resurgence of some sort of "neo-fascist" tendency in American politics or in the West. That element was there from the foundation of the country and it is deeply rooted in Western tradition. The Nazi preoccupation with eugenics and racial superiority was always an element of American society; a society which outlawed interracial relations, and which marginalized mixed race individuals to reinforce this racial caste system. A racial caste system developed throughout the Americas.

Nazi Germany and the United States both shared the common belief that Europeans were a superior race. This was demonstrated during World War II. In *Black Power*, Stokely Carmichael (also known as Kwame Ture) and Charles Hamilton write: "This country also saw fit to treat German prisoners of war more humanely than it treated its own black soldiers. On one occasion, a group of black soldiers was transporting German prisoners by train through the South to a prisoner-of-war camp. The railroad diner required the black American soldiers eat in segregated facilities on the train—only four at a time and with considerable delay—while the German prisoners (white, of course) ate without delay and with other passengers in the main section of the diner!"

I present all of this at the onset so that one clearly understands my position as it relates to Western civilization. I view Western civilization through the lens of a victim of that civilization, not as a defender of Western civilization, so I certainly cannot share the alarm and concern that is expressed by Donald Trump and Patrick Buchanan. Moreover, I also will add that my position is that Western civilization does indeed face a crisis, but that this is a self-inflicted crisis, although Trump and Buchanan obviously do not present it as such. Trump speaks of those who seek to destroy Western civilization, but historically the biggest threat to Western civilization has been itself. Buchanan himself exposes as much, which is actually the focus of my review.

Buchanan's view is that the large influx of immigrants coming into America is a threat to American civilization. To support this view he quotes Peter Heath, who wrote:

"In 376 a large band of Gothic refugees arrived at the Empire's Danube frontier, asking for asylum. In a complete break with established Roman policy, they were allowed in, unsubdued. They revolted, and within two years had defeated and killed the emperor Valens-the one who had received them-along with two-thirds of his army, at the battle of Hadrianople."

Based on this passage, Buchanan explains:

"What Valens had done was the Christian thing to do, but it had never been the Roman thing to do. Valens has his modern counterpart in George W. Bush. For in May 2006, Republican· senators at Bush's urging joined Democrats to offer a blanket amnesty to 12 million illegal aliens. and permit U.S. businesses to go abroad and bring in foreign workers. Senators had been shocked by the millions of Hispanics marching in America's cities under Mexican flags. And as was the emperor Valens, President Bush was hailed for his compassion and vision."

Buchanan argues that the fall of Rome was the result of Rome becoming a multicultural society that incorporated foreigners who did not assimilate Roman values. This was perhaps one aspect of why Rome fell, but Buchanan also admits that the "barbarians" who conquered Rome were themselves conquered by Rome in the past:

"But these alien peoples brought with them no reverence for Roman gods, no respect for Roman tradition, no love of Roman culture. And so, as Rome had conquered the barbarians, the barbarians conquered Rome. In the fifth century, beginning with Alaric and the Visigoths in 410, the northern tribes, one after another, invaded and sacked the Eternal City. And the Dark Ages descended."

Buchanan is worried that America and Europe will suffer a similar fate to that of Rome in that the people who were formerly enslaved and colonized will invade Western civilization and gradually erode the values of that civilization. It is the concerns of people like Buchanan that was one of the reasons why Trump was elected. Trump understood the fears and insecurities that white society has over the threat that Western civilization faces, which was the message of the previously mentioned speech which Trump delivered in Poland.

An aspect of Western civilization's fragility is the ever present need to defend itself, whether militarily or morally. This is why Buchanan writes:

"Colonial rule was marked by such evils as chattel slavery and the exploitation of African labor in the mines of the Congo and South Africa. But was not the arrival of the West of immense benefit to the colonized peoples? Can Western civilization not Claim credit for having advanced all of mankind morally, politically, culturally between 1492 and 1960? Was not Western civilization vastly superior to the indigenous civilizations it encountered and crushed) from the Aztecs and Incas in the Americas to the Muslim, Hindu, Buddhist, Taoist civilizations from Africa to the Far East? Has not Western Man more to be proud of than ashamed of?"

This passage demonstrates the defensive nature of the West. Buchanan cannot merely state that slavery and colonialism were wrong, but he has to also offer a defense of Western civilization by speaking of the supposed good things that came out of colonization. The argument is essentially that slavery was bad, but that the West is still morally and culturally superior to the people that it murdered. What type of moral superiority is that? What type of culture is that?

Certainly, one finds warfare in Africa, but the destructive impulse that drives Western civilization was rarely to be found in Africa. One scholar writes of Africa's history: "Throughout their history, with the possible exception of the armies of Shaka Zulu, Africans had observed limits to the use of violence, sometimes even substituting ritual and symbol for physical force." But the morally superior Western world invaded Africa and committed several acts of genocide. This was done in the name of religion and civilization. It is noticeable that Buchanan attempts to downplay the worst aspects of colonialism, such as the millions that were massacred in Africa by European colonialists.

Buchanan also expresses issues with the United Nations conference which was held in South Africa in 2001: "In the first week of September 2001, in Durban, South Africa, a UN World Conference Against Racism, Racial Discrimination, Xenophobia and Related Intolerance was held. It quickly degenerated into an anti-white, anti-Western, anti-Israel jamboree. At the end a demand was made on the United States for reparations for the transatlantic slave trade."

Buchanan's view of world history is one in which the West has always been benevolent to the Third World. The various Western supported coups that toppled democratically elected governments around the world are not mentioned by Buchanan. Moreover, Buchanan complains that "Islamic nations that perpetuated slavery into the modern era, long after the Christian West had brought the evil to an end, were exempted from the reparations demands." Buchanan is oblivious to the fact that those who were raising the demands for reparations at the U.N. conference included activists such as Edna Roland, who descends from Africans who were enslaved by Europeans in Brazil. In other words, there was a specific reason for why Western countries were the target of the reparations claim during this conference.

The reason by Buchanan spends so much time in his book

trying to defend the West or downplay the West's history of aggression against other people is because he fears that Western societies, particularly America, will become ashamed of its own history:

"Nor do Americans treasure the history or revere the heroes as we once did. What many still see as a glorious past, others see as shameful history. Columbus, Washington, Jefferson, Jackson, Lincoln, and Lee, heroes of the old America, are all under attack. To many, the discovery of America by the explorers from Columbus to Captain John Smith, and the winning of the West by pioneers, soldiers, and cowboys are no longer seen as heroic events but as matters of which Western man should be ashamed."

I do not think Western man needs to be ashamed, but let's be honest about the crimes committed by Western man against other people around the world. Buchanan writes: "Western society is afflicted with a guilty conscience. For Europeans, the guilt is over centuries of imperial rule. For Americans, it is guilt over our ancestors' injustices to the Native Americans and two centuries of enslavement of black Americans, followed by a century of segregation."

Buchanan is less concerned with the impact that Western imperialism has had on its victims and is instead concerned about this guilty conscience. He continues: "Our ancestors were not paralyzed by guilt. Confident in their culture and civilization, they believed in their superiority over what Kipling had called the 'lesser breeds without the law.' We come from a different people than the people we have become." Buchanan does not hesitant to acknowledge that President Andrew Jackson was a slave owner who viewed Native Americans as savages, that President Abraham Lincoln believed in white supremacy, or that Woodrow Wilson was a segregationist. Buchanan explains that "if racism means a belief in the superiority of the white race and its inherent right to rule other peoples, American history is full of such men."

Buchanan seems troubled that Westerners would look at their history of genocide, colonialism, and slavery with anything less than reverence. One issue that is apparent in his book is that Buchanan is incapable of viewing the world from the lens of those who were oppressed by Western civilization. He writes: "Growing up in the 1940s and 1950s, we did not feel any need to apologize

33

for America's past, but took pride in all she had accomplished. African-Americans shared that pride." The 1950s was when the civil rights movement took off. African Americans at the time could not vote, go to an integrated school, or even drink from the same water fountain as white people, so one struggles to find this shared pride that Buchanan refers to.

One must give Buchanan some credit, however. He does not attempt to hide or cover up the racist nature of Western civilization. Instead, he argues that the technological and other advancements of the West offset the negatives. He complains that "though the achievements of our civilization in art, architecture, law, literature, technology, science, and governance, and the advance of human freedom and God-given rights eclipse those of any other, there has arisen among our intellectual and cultural elites a contempt for the West. Many see our ancestors as irredeemably racist, imperialist, and genocidal."

It is indeed true that over the last 500 years Western civilization has been one that has made many great advancements, but often at the cost of great human suffering. Buchanan attempts to maintain the curious position of trying to assert that Westerners should not feel ashamed of their history of imperialism, while also asserting the moral superiority and Christian values of the West. Which is it? Is Western civilization a morally superior civilization that places value on Christian ideals of peace and brotherhood, or is it a civilization that has no guilt for the destruction that it has caused? Buchanan boasts that Europeans were men "who went out from Europe to conquer and Christianize the world" because he wants to uphold both positions. In doing so, Buchanan provides support to an argument which was put forward by the psychologist Dr. Bobby E. Wright.

In his book, *The Psychopathic Racial Personality and Other Essays*, Dr. Bobby E. Wright presents Western civilization as a psychopathic civilization. Wright writes that because "of their lack of ethical or moral development there is no conflict between" Western religion and racism. Wright continues to explain that Europeans have "historically oppressed, exploited, and killed Black people, all in the name of their God Jesus Christ and with the sanction of their churches." Buchanan's attempts to defend Western civilization proves Wright's point that white people "have no mortality where race is the variable."

I also turn to another psychologist, Amos Wilson. In *The Falsification of Afrikan Consciousness: Eurocentric History, Psychiatry and the Politics of White Supremacy*, he criticized what he saw as the apparent normalization of European imperialism: "We know that imperialist Europeans stole nations and destroyed hundreds of thousands of Amerindians, Afrikans, and other peoples; and whose every step in other people's nations has done little but destroy the local people, drive them out of their minds, destroy their cultures, and rob them of their wealth. And yet, these people are held up as normal..."

In his book, Buchanan also mentions the controversy that emerged in France in 2005 when a law was enacted, which mandated that "school programs recognize in particular the positive character of the French overseas presence, notably in North Africa." The fact that Algeria fought a bloody war against France for their independence would suggest that Algerians certainly did not view French colonialism as something positive. Frantz Fanon came to support the struggle of the Algerian people when he saw how horribly they were being treated. President Abdelaziz Bouteflika of Algeria was not pleased by this new law. He said that the French "have no choice but to recognize that they tortured, killed, exterminated from 1830 to 1962," but Buchanan is not concerned with viewing the history of French colonialism in North Africa from the perspective of the Algerian victims. Buchanan explains: "But the ultimate issue here is not what foreigners or immigrants think of the history of France. The issue is what the French think, and whether the children of France shall be taught that their nation's history is glorious or sordid." Again, Buchanan only wants to view the world through the perspective of Europeans and not those who were oppressed by European colonialism.

Buchanan also expresses little interest in the cultures of non-Western people. Buchanan writes that in the 1960, African Americans "were not fully integrated into society, but they had been assimilated into our culture." He also writes: "We were of two races, but of one nationality: Americans." Buchanan fails to understand that this shared culture was not so much assimilation, but imposition. African Americans were enslaved and had Western culture imposed on them. Therefore, it seems to trouble Buchanan when he sees apparent rejections of Western culture on the part of African American who are seeking to reconnect with their African heritage. This is why he writes: "In the 1960s, black leaders from basketball great Lew Alcindor to boxing legend Cassius Clay, to poet Leroi Jones, to radicals like H. Rap Brown and Stokely Carmichael, began to adopt African and Islamic names to stress the degrees of separation from an American Christian mainstream."

Buchanan also references Shelby Steele, who explained: "No group in recent history has more aggressively seized power in the name of its racial superiority than Western whites. This race illustrated for all time-through colonialism, slavery, white racism, Nazism-the extraordinary evil that follows when great power is joined to an atavistic sense of superiority and destiny. This is why today's whites the world over, cannot openly have a racial identity."

Steele continues to explain: "Black children today are hammered with the idea of racial identity and pride, yet racial pride in whites constitutes a grave evil. Say 'I'm white and I'm proud,' and you are a Nazi." I would argue that this is a bit of an exaggeration to suggest that white pride is necessarily seen as being evil. This is not a position that I maintain, but I will concede that Steele does have a point. The difference is, however, that the same legacy of racial superiority which Steele acknowledges is precisely why racial identity for white people is not the same as it is for black people. People such as Buchanan actually make it difficult for white people to assert a positive racial identity because he upholds the racists and takes the position that Westerners should not be ashamed to revere these racist imperialists. It is people like Buchanan who help to create the perception that racial pride among white people promotes racism.

Buchanan writes that "if black children are being 'hammered with the idea of racial identity and pride,' the 'color-blind society' of Dr. King's dream is dead." The problem is that Western society never accepted King's dream, which is why King endured being jailed on numerous occasions before he was finally assassinated. Given the manner in which Buchanan writes about Western history, I wonder if he even truly believes in King's dream.

I opened this piece by referencing Trump's remarks in Poland.

As I have noted, both Trump and Buchanan share a common concern over the future of Western civilization. The central premise of *State of Emergency* is this need to protect the West from what Buchanan sees as an invasion.

It is ironic that Buchanan expresses so much concern about protecting America's borders and rule of law, when those were the very things which Europeans undermined when they went to Africa. Contrary to how African history is sometimes presented, the rule of law did exist in Africa. Chancellor Williams gave the following description of how elders handled disputes in chiefless African societies. He writes: "Matters involving members of the same family or clan could be settled by the family council, each family or clan having its own elder. Conflicts between families or clans could be brought before any mutually acceptable elder for settlement. The elder's judgment was not binding on the parties to the dispute. [...] If the case was 'big' and serious and the disputants were dissatisfied with the elder's decision regarding it, they could call in one or more additional elders to hear and pass on the case." Williams points out that the elder's decisions were "advisory." This meant that the elders' judgment could be ignored, though Williams adds that "to ignore the elders was considered to be ignoring the community itself."

The king was also someone who maintained law and order. The absence of a king meant the absence of such law and order. Walter Rodney explained: "The intimate link between the king and the concept of law is demonstrated by the fact that the absence of a king, as in the interval between the death of one king and the crowning of the next, usually meant disorder and lawlessness." Rodney notes that during the period of civil strife over succession, the Papels of the Upper Guinea coast were known to have engaged in acts of robbery. Nicholas Owen, who was a slave dealer, recorded in 1757 that he heard news that the king of Sherbro was dead, but this news had not spread abroad because of the custom of keeping the death of a king hidden in order to make a new king "before any trouble ensues." Those last words were what Owen himself wrote. If there was no king present, then there was trouble.

In some cases, laws were represented by clan elders or by the king in societies with rulers. Maintaining law and order was sometimes a very delicate task because of the authority vested in certain figures and if that authority figure were to die, there would be no law and order until that position was replaced.

Western society has never been one to respect the borders or social orders of our civilizations. We see this in West Africa with Kwame Ansa, an African chief who responded to the Portuguese request to build a fortress on his land by saying that "it is far preferable that both our nations should continue on the same footing as they have hitherto done, allowing your ships to come and go as usual; the desire of seeing each other occasionally will preserve peace between us." Kwame Ansa recognized the potential for conflict if the Europeans attempted to settle in African lands and Ansa wanted to maintain the peace by keeping Europeans at a distance.

The Portuguese who came into West Africa demonstrated a disregard for many of the local laws and customs. Walter Rodney writes that "European traders took greatest exception to those African laws which had a direct bearing on European property." These laws stipulated that if a European trader died then his host would inherit the trader's property. This was a common law in the Upper Guinea Coast of West Africa. For example, if an animal fell dead in the domain of a specific ruler that ruler could then claim the animal, even if the animal was wounded outside of his territory by hunters who were not his subjects. Mansa Felupe, an African king, inherited the goods of all who died in his kingdom, as well as the property of his subjects that died in a foreign land. Walter Rodney explains that the Portuguese settlers "made strenuous attempts to change the nature of the agreements and to escape, in one way or another, from the authority of the African rulers."

The attempt to undermine the authority of the African rulers sometimes led to the instigation of conflicts between Africans. For example, some of the Portuguese who were living among the Banhun people were frustrated by the fact that they were being mistreated by the Banhun people. They invoked the support of King Masatamba, who attacked the Banhuns. The lack of regard for African customs and way of life was also demonstrated by Louis Binger, a French explorer. Binger said, and I quote: "I feel that a white man traveling in this country, whoever he may be, should not prostrate himself before a black king, however powerful the latter may be." He continued to explain that Europeans should "not have to bow their heads before indigenous chiefs to whom they are definitely superior in all respects." Europeans came into Africa as conquerors. They had no respect for the customs, laws, or territorial space of the people that they invaded.

Western civilization is one that has been very brutal in its conquests of others and seems to have a fear of falling victim to a similar type of invasion, but the reality is that much of the threats that Western civilization has faced has been self-inflicted. As Buchanan explained, it was other Europeans who destroyed Rome, but we can observe this pattern throughout Europe's history. The Greek city-states of Athens and Sparta fought a very brutal war against each other, known as the Peloponnesian War.

There were also the self-inflicted World Wars. Buchanan writes: "By 1918, the German, Austro-Hungarian, and Russian empires had collapsed. World War II bled and broke the British and French." These changes were caused not by invaders from the "Third World," but by Europeans fighting each other over global control over the world. The topic of World War returns us back to Trump's speech.

Trump framed his speech in Poland around this notion of defending Western civilization from threats. But what becomes apparent from listening to that speech is that much of the threat that Poland has faced was from other European people, other white people. Trump said: "In 1920, in the Miracle of Vistula, Poland stopped the Soviet army bent on European conquest. Then, 19 years later in 1939, you were invaded yet again, this time by Nazi Germany from the west and the Soviet Union from the east. That's trouble. That's tough."

Poland stopped an invasion from the Soviet Union and then nearly twenty years later was invaded by the Nazis. Trump is right. That is tough. These are white people fighting white people here. That is the trouble that Trump is referring to. Trump continues:

"Under a double occupation the Polish people endured evils beyond description: the Katyn forest massacre, the occupations, the Holocaust, the Warsaw Ghetto and the Warsaw Ghetto Uprising, the destruction of this beautiful capital city, and the deaths of nearly one in five Polish people. A vibrant Jewish population—the largest in Europe—was reduced to almost nothing after the Nazis systematically murdered millions of Poland's Jewish citizens, along with countless others, during that brutal occupation."

The imperialistic and destructive nature of Western civilization has not only been a danger to others, but it has been a danger to itself as well. Underneath this death and destruction is also a deep-seated feeling of inferiority and insecurity, which I have discussed at length. I will make reference to Marcus Garvey because Garvey clearly understood that the racism and oppression which African people experienced was rooted in this fear on the part of Europeans of losing their civilization to other people—precisely the same fear that Buchanan expressed in his book and that Trump expressed in his speech.

Garvey explained:

"Should you reverse the positions you would do the same thing as they did to us. Why do I say that? There is no man in this hall tonight—no Negro man or woman in this hall tonight—because all of us are human—who would for a whole life time labor and work himself industrially and thriftily to save everything that you possibly can to build up a home of your own and save a little fortune of your own to make yourself happy, and that after you did all that—you have your children; you have your own family to take care of and to look after with that which you individually worked for—there is no one of you who would go out into the street and see a tramp and take that tramp and bring him into your house and let him sleep in the same bed with you; let him occupy your drawing-room, let him enjoy all the comforts of it, and later on have him say to you, 'Let me tell you how to run your house.' There is no human being in this building who would do that. Yet that is what we expect the white man to do [...]."

What Garvey was explaining is that it is not realistic to expect white people to simply give their power to us. This desire to hold on to white domination in America is at the core of white supremacist thinking. Organizations such as the Ku Klux Klan and the Neo-Nazis reason that America is a country that was colonized and built by white people for white people, and they are not wrong in this view. The native people of the Americas were merely an obstacle to the building of this country. They had to be driven away so that the white colonizers could take their land. As for African people, we were the slave labor. That was the dynamic that founded this country. It was a country created by white people for white people.

The United States is a country that was founded on the principle of liberty, but there was never a doubt that this principle was intended for white people, especially wealthy white people. As such, African people have typically been on our own when it comes to engaging in certain struggles for equal rights. This was one of the issues that we saw in the American labor movement, which was really just a white labor movement. This was why in 1959 the black members of the American Federation of Labor and Congress of Industrial Organizations (AFL–CIO) had to form their own Negro American Labor Council (NALC) under the leadership of A. Philip Randolph. Randolph complained: "It is unfortunate that some of our liberal friends, along with some of the leaders of labor, even yet do not comprehend the nature, scope, depth, and challenge of this civil rights revolution which is surging forward in the House of Labor." The reality is that when you look at American history, you will find numerous examples of the white working class struggling for their own advancement with little regard to the struggles of African people.

When we look at what has taken place in America over the last ten years, we can understand why certain elements in the country are behaving as they are. First there was the economic collapse in 2008, in which many people lost their jobs and their houses. Economic insecurity is one of the pillars on which Donald Trump built his campaign. There are many white people in this country who are frustrated with their condition. They have lost their jobs and they feel as though they are losing their country. They witnessed the election of a black man named Barack Obama. Even worse than that, this was a black man with a Kenyan father and a white mother. White supremacist organizations like the Ku Klux Klan and the Nazis were always preoccupied with purity of blood, so it must have been an especially stinging blow to see a black man with a white mother take over the presidency of their country—as it is no doubt a blow to see Colin Kaepernick, another black man with a white mother, kneel to American anthem.

I do not sympathize with the Neo-Nazis and other white nationalist organizations that share their philosophies, but I understand their position and I understand their frustration. I reiterate that as far as these people are concerned America was founded by their white ancestors and they refuse to give up that country without a struggle. I quote Marcus Garvey again:

"Prejudice we shall always have between black and white, so long as the latter believes that the former is intruding upon their rights. So long as white laborers believe that black laborers are taking and holding their jobs, so long as white artisans believe that black artisans are performing the work that they should do; so long as white men and women believe that black men and women are filling the positions that they covet; so long as white political leaders and statesmen believe that black politicians and statesmen are seeking the same positions in the nation's government; so long as white men believe that black men want to associate with and marry white women, then we will ever have prejudice, and only prejudice, but riots, lynchings, burnings, and God to tell what next will follow!"

This insecurity and this fear of losing power is one of the things that drove white racists to commit the atrocities against African people that they did, which is why Garvey's words here are so profound. Garvey understood that the European powers have no interest in sharing power or sharing wealth with African people. This same insecurity and fear are also one of the reasons why Trump was elected.

In conclusion, I will state that I agree with Buchanan's premise that Western civilization is in a state of emergency, but I would argue that this emergency is a self-inflicted one, not an emergency that was created by the "Third World" which Buchanan fears so much.

Response from the first critic: You speak at length about how European society is built from exploitation and oppression. I do not deny this, but my question to you is how do you reconcile your critical position on Western civilization with the reality that slavery existed in Africa before Europeans colonized Africa? What would you also say about the fact that it was Europeans who actually abolished slavery in Africa?

You pretend to be morally superior to Patrick Buchanan, but in reality your position is just as racist as his is because you are clearly trying to paint the picture that white people (Western civilization) are all racists and that we are so violent that white people are a threat to each other, but you say very little about the tribal wars and the massacres in Africa.

Slavery was terrible, but the slave trade could not have happened if Africans did not participate in it as well. We need to stop judging things based on race and judge each other as individuals. There were both blacks and whites who were at fault in slavery, and whites and blacks who fought to end it. Likewise, there were white people who were involved in the civil rights movement. Whites are not all evil and neither is Western civilization. Also, Africans are not all saints either.

Eddie Wilson's response: Let me begin by clearly expressing my view that I do not look at the world in terms of inferior or superior people or civilizations. Unlike Buchanan, my position is not rooted in fear of some imaginary invasion or threat to African people—I don't have to imagine a threat because as African people we live this threat daily. Secondly, I don't believe that a person is inherently good or inherently bad because of their racial background. This means that I do not discount white people who are genuinely good people, but it is my contention that such people will be open and honest about the crimes that their people have committed against African people.

As for what you stated regarding slavery, my response to this is that slavery in Africa is not what it was in the Americas. This is not a defense of any type of slavery or system in which one human becomes subservient to another. The fact is that what my ancestors experienced over in the Americas was a system that was very dehumanizing and the only way for my ancestors to advance was to fight this system, and eventually destroy it. What you find in Africa was that slaves were not in a fixed position of servitude. It is not unheard of to find examples of slaves or children of slaves becoming important rulers in African society. A slave in African societies often also had legal rights as well. The constitution of Mali, for example, stated: "Do not ill treat the slaves. We are the master of the slave but not the bag he carries." The American Supreme Court, on the other hand, ruled that slaves were not accorded the rights of an American citizen.

Let me give you an example. This is about a Yoruba king known as Atiba. According to tradition, Atiba was born to a slave mother who was given to the King of Oyo as a hostage. Atiba's mother had a very close friend who could not bear to be separated from her friend, so she decided to return to the city to visit her friend. She went about the city asking for her friend, who was one of the king's wives. This caught the king's attention and he invited her to explain her reason for being in his kingdom. She came before the king, King Abiodun, and explained to him that the woman that was given to him as a hostage was her friend and that she had come to visit her friend.

The king, testing this woman's resolve, asked her if she was not afraid that he would add her to his harem, kill her, or sell her away. Her response was that she was willing to undergo any treatment for the sake of her friend. She even explained that she would have no problem being made a wife of the king because it meant that she would see her friend. The king was so impressed that he allowed her to stay with her friend. The king eventually sent the two women home, with the woman that had been given to him as a hostage pregnant with his child. Before they departed, the king gave them some presents, and he made them both his deputies. He put these women in charge of making decisions in all matters that related to Oyo and all of the tribute money was to be paid to them.

These women returned to Gudugbu where they became important rulers. The king's wife eventually gave birth to a son, who was named Atiba. Consider the events thus far. Atiba's mother was a slave woman who was brought to the king as a hostage, yet she was made one of his chief deputies in the district of the kingdom in which she lived, and tribute money was given to her. Now, you find me any examples where an enslaved African woman in the Americas rose to such power. Even white women during this period of time could scarcely hope to be placed in such a position of influence.

Atiba grew up to be a very wild and reckless boy. One story tells that he was chastised by his maternal uncle because he had asked his uncle for a yam. His uncle explained to Atiba that he would not have gotten any yam if he lived the idle life of raiding that Atiba lived. Atiba was someone who amassed his wealth through raids. Atiba became so popular that upon the death of King Oluewu, the crown was passed to Atiba, the child of a slave. After he became king, Atiba moved the capital from Oyo to Ago, which was renamed as Oyo, or also known as "Ago which became Oyo." Atiba enjoyed a long and peaceful reign, which was marked by checking the incursions being made by the Fulani. He died an old man in 1859.

The reason why I wanted to go into those details about Atiba is that he is one of Oyo's greatest rulers, and he was the child of a slave woman. That same slave woman also became a very important political personality in the kingdom. So, I do recognize that forms of exploitation did exist in Africa, but not on the same scale as what was happening in Western society. Had Atiba been enslaved in the United States or the Caribbean, he could never have hoped to have risen to the position that he did.

Critic: Your response is very typical of you Pan-African racists who only want to blame white people for all of the world's problems. You claim that you are not defending slavery, but then try to draw a comparison which makes slavery in Africa look favorable because Atiba was able to go from being a slave to a ruler. I think you give your own ancestors far too little credit. George Washington Carver was a slave who became a prominent scientist and Booker T. Washington rose up from slavery to become one of America's most renown educators. Frederick Douglass was also a slave as well. It is not as though African Americans were not able to rise up from slavery and accomplish great things in America, but they certainly could not do so by blaming the white man for their conditions. And slavery could not have been ended in America if not for the help of white people. Never forget that!

I am against any form of racial separatism or segregation, and this is what you seem to be preaching. You seem to only concern yourself with African people, even though you are not an African yourself. You were born in America and you should be a proud American. America does have its faults, but no nation is perfect. I believe, as Dr. King believed, America has to be perfected, but this can only be done if American citizens put aside our differences and work to make our country great again.

With Trump in office we finally have that chance. We have a president who truly loves our country and who does not divide us with racial identity politics like Obama did. That is what Patrick Buchanan is writing about as well. We have to stop dividing our nation and unite. This means celebrating the contributions that were made by all Americans, including African Americans.

Whether you like it or not, you are an American as well.

A response from a second critic: I think your views on Western civilization are very unfortunate. You strike me as being no different from the Nation of Islam and all of the other anti-Semitic black hate cults. For all I know, you probably have no issue with the atrocities that befell the Jews because, as you claim, it was merely the chickens coming home to roost. This is how you so callously describe the holocaust, the murder, the slaughter of six million people. You make such a big deal of Europeans slaughtering others, but you are so indifferent Jewish life that it is appalling and makes no better than Buchanan.

Why did you fail to acknowledge the slavery in Egypt? Is it because you know that you Africans were the original oppressors of the Jewish people? Is it because acknowledging the racial oppression of the Jews in Egypt ruins your victimhood narrative? Was the enslavement of African Americans chickens coming home to roost for what Egyptians did to Jews? Afrocentric racists like yourself are always distorting history to make yourselves into the victims, but the truth is that Africans were not all so innocent as you try to make it seem.

Westerners also helped to bring the values of Western enlightenment and Christianity to Africa. Before Western colonialism, Africans were engaged in barbaric practices such as human sacrifices and the infanticide of twins. As even you have had to acknowledge, Africans did participate in the slave trade. The reason why they did so is because African societies at the time were already engaged in tribal wars which resulted in the enslavement of those who were captured. African chiefs thought so little of their captives that few hesitated to trade away the captives for European goods, which Africans were incapable of producing for themselves.

I know you will accuse me of racism, but it was the superior military, political, and moral position of the West which allowed us to conquer Africa. Africans were very easily enticed into selling their own into slavery and were very easily set off against each other because Africans had not yet reached the stage of political development to overcome petty tribal differences. Tribalism still is an issue in Africa today.

Slavery is also still an issue in much of Africa today. You may complain about Western slavery, but the West led the world in abolishing the evil practice of slavery. Can you please show me where in Africa was there a strong abolitionist movement to suppress the trade in other humans?

The final point that I must note is that you criticize Western civilization, yet you do so through an English language which is Western and through the medium of writing which was introduced to your ancestors by way of the West. You are the typical example of an Afrocentric extremist who is at once thoroughly Westernized, yet you use your Westernization to deride the West. This may seem like a bit of a cliché, but my question is if you detest the West so much, why not go to Africa and see how well-off Africans are without the refinements of Western civilization.

Eddie Wilson: The point that you make about Jewish slavery in Egypt is not a new one. Antenor Firmin made a similar point, writing: "As he reviews the past he will remember that there was a time when the savage Tamahov and the humble Amov, the children of Seth and Japheth were themselves under the harsh rule of his Black ancestors. The gigantic monuments which are the glory of Egypt had been built with the labor of Whites from the East and the West. Humanity is one in time as it is in space; the injustices of past centuries echo those of the present centuries."

I disagree. The point Firmin was intending to make is the same one you are trying to make; which is to suggest that the injustices that Africans endured by Europeans is some sort of karma for what the Egyptians did to the Hebrews. Even if we assume that the Bible's narrative of the Exodus story is meant to convey a historical account rather than a mere fable, then we will have to acknowledge that it was not the original position of the Egyptians to oppress the Hebrews. It was the pharaoh who knew not Joseph who began the oppression of the Hebrews.

I mention this because it is clear that the Egyptians did not have any sort of racial prejudice against the Hebrews and, as Sigmund Freud argued, it was from the Egyptians that the Hebrew people may have acquired their religious practices in the first place. Moreover, it was Africans who saved the Hebrews from an Assyrian invasion, so African people have given much to the Jewish people, so do not try to use the mythical Hebrew enslavement in Egypt to support your unfounded claim that I am anti-Semitic, when anti-Jewish bigotry is so firmly rooted in Western civilization that you don't even want to confront it.

The religious values of which you speak of have always been a sham. European societies have never wanted to be constrained to the moral teachings of their own religious doctrines. We can start with the fact that it was the Romans (Europeans) who killed Christ in the first place. Then when Christianity began to spread in Europe, the Romans violently suppressed the Christians. I am sure you know this history better than I do, but my point is that Europeans themselves have a very bloody history where Christianity is concerned.

What is also worth noting here is that European interest in Africa was sparked by rumors of a Christian king in Ethiopia known as Prester John. The rumors claimed that this African king had slaughtered his Muslim foes and was willing to assist Europe in its holy crusades against the Muslims. There were also rumors that Prester John was in Asia. No one knew where he was or how to reach him, but I think it is worth noting that prior to the European invasion of Africa, Africa was seen as the potential homeland of this great Christian ruler who was to help save Christianity. European Christians were looking to Africa for inspiration in the faith, not the other way around.

You also have some nerve to accuse me of anti-Semitism, while also trying to highlight the glories of Western civilization. The first ghettos in Europe were built for Jewish people. The Holocaust was carried out in Europe. Jews were also persecuted during the Crusades. Europe has a long history of anti-Jewish sentiment. Hatred of Jewish people comes from your civilization, not mine.

Remember that the time when Jesus was born, Jews were living under the domination of Rome. Jews revolted on numerous occasions. One of these revolts was led by Simon bar Kokhba. This is your history; your Western history. It is the Roman Empire, which you take such pride in, that destroyed the Jewish homeland in the first place. You can cite the Bible as a reference to Jewish slavery in Egypt, but the Egyptians allowed Israel to flourish. Nowhere in the Bible does one read about an African civilization attacking and destroying Israel, so hatred of Jews is part of your culture, not mine.

What you say is true. There is slavery in Africa today, but I am sure that is little of your concern. You only mention it so that you can feel morally superior, but you care very little about the suffering of Africans who do experience slavery. I say this with confidence because the criminal justice system in America enslaves African people—read the Constitution—and you would not condemn slavery in your own nation, but you point to Africa to escape facing the immorality of your own justice system. Furthermore, you want to run me back to Africa so that you will not have to confront the truths that I have been saying.

6 THE REVOLUTION IN NAMIBIA

Herman Andimba Toivo ya Toivo, who was one of the leading figures in Namibia's fight for independence, passed in June 2017. In this article, Eddie Wilson reflects on some of the failures of the revolutionary struggle which Toivo ya Toivo was involved in.

When I saw the news that Herman Andimba Toivo ya Toivo died, I began to reflect on the fact that yet another revolutionary fighter from the era of the anti-colonial war in southern Africa has passed and leaves behind so much unfinished work. This is not unlike my reaction to Mandela's passing. We celebrate these great ancestors for their commitment to struggle and the sacrifices that they endured, yet one cannot help but question if these ancestors fought hard enough. Had they done enough to prepare us for liberation?

Toivo was the co-founder of the Ovamboland People's Organisation (OPO), which was organized against South Africa's occupation of Namibia. OPO eventually became the South West African People's Organization (SWAPO). Namibia was a German colony, but South Africa was granted trusteeship of the territory after World War I. After World War II, South Africa refused to allow Namibia, then known as South West Africa, to become independent.

For his political activities, Toivo was imprisoned on Robben Island, along with Nelson Mandela. At his trial in 1967, Toivo defended his decision to take up arms to defend his people. He explained: "Violence is truly fearsome, but who would not defend his property and himself against a robber?" Toivo was no stranger to fighting wars. In 1942, pro-Nazi settlers were plotting to reconquer the colony. Toivo volunteered for the South African Native Military Corps. to protect his homeland from a Nazi occupation. Toivo was sure to mention this fact in his trial. The judge who was presiding over the case labeled Toivo as a coward, to which Toivo remarked: "I volunteered to face German bullets, and as a guard of military installations, both in South West Africa and the republic, I was prepared to be the victim of their sabotage. Today, they are our masters and are considered the heroes, and I am called the coward."

Toivo put on a very courageous display. He was sentenced to twenty years in jail, but his statements were read abroad and helped to influence international opinion. Toivo remained defiant in prison and on one occasion smacked one of the warders, which resulted in Toivo being sent to solitary confinement. Tovio was released in 1984 and continued the fight until 1990, when Namibia became independent.

After Namibia was given its independence in 1990, after a long and brutal struggle for freedom, are the people of Namibia free? Toivo, like so many others in the struggle against European domination in southern Africa, was imprisoned for his role in the struggle. After Namibia gained its independence, Toivo served in the government of Sam Nujoma.

Much like how the African National Congress has been the only political party to rule in South Africa since the end of apartheid, SWAPO is currently the only political party to rule in Namibia and what has the result of that rule been? Namibia, like South Africa, is still a poor country in which the political elites are well off as the average people struggle. Once apartheid ended, many of those who fought apartheid came to enrich themselves. The mentality of many of these freedom fighters was to drive the Europeans out of political power so that they could enrich themselves.

Much like South Africa, Namibia has also faced issues regarding land. Under colonial rule, there was an unequal distribution of land between Africans and Europeans. This unequal distribution persisted even after independence. A few years ago, the Affirmative Repositioning Movement was formed as an organization seeking to address this issue under the leadership of Job Amupanda. This movement submitted more than 50,000 land applications through authorities. The Affirmative Repositioning Movement made it clear that if government officials were not willing to address the issue then the Affirmative Repositioning Movement would pursue further action, whether legal or not. Amupanda accused government officials of not seriously addressing the issue. When interviewed about the issue, Amupanda stated that "people who are sleeping in garages have no peace. People without houses have no peace."

Toivo ya Toivo should be commended for his role in the liberation struggle, but what next? African revolutionary leaders from the 1960s through the 1990s demonstrated that they were effective at taking power, but the challenge has been what to do once power has been obtained. Unlike many other African nations, Namibia has not had to endure brutal military dictatorships, coups, or civil wars for power. Despite this, Namibia, much like South Africa, has still wrestled with inequality and political corruption on the part of a political leadership which has been content to enrich itself as the people suffer. Independence for Namibia led to the emergence of a new black middle class and a political elite. The rural masses have experienced little material benefits following independence.

The problem is very clear, but what would the solution have been? What could have been done differently? This is something that African nations have struggled with following independence. Independence from colonial rule typically meant the advancement of a small African elite, but the masses remained in a state of poverty. As Amupanda pointed out, government officials in Namibia spoke of maintaining the peace because they enjoy a type of peace which the poor and suffering masses of Namibia are not able to enjoy.

I mention Amupanda not only because he is a Namibian activist who challenged the unequal land distribution in Namibia, but he also presented a model for which Namibia should look to in order to develop its economy. Amupanda writes: "Namibia not only has high levels of poverty, unemployment and inequality, the country has one of the highest records of economic inequality in the whole world." He points out that what the Namibian leaders have done since independence has failed and he offers China as a model.

Amupanda explains that China is important to Africa's development because China has a policy of non-intervention, unlike Western governments. Therefore, Chinese financial aid is usually given to African countries without any "good governance" or human rights strings attached—although, Western governments typically ignore human rights abuses by African dictators whenever it is in their interest to do so.

Apart from this, as I noted, Amupanda sees China as a model for Namibia because of the economic reforms which were undertaken in China under the leadership of Deng Xiaoping. Amupanda notes that whereas Deng has been criticized for the autocratic nature of his government, scholars hardly fault Deng's economic policies which transformed Chin from a poor former colony of Japan to one of the most powerful economic powers in the world. This transformation was accomplished through market reforms which allowed certain cities to pursue a free market path and to attract foreign investment. Amupanda is also cautious to point out that there are certain aspects of China which Africa should avoid adopting. He quotes Mabasa and Mqolomba, who caution against "negative trends such as authoritarianism and persistent inequality should not be replicated."

Amupanda contrasts China's development with Namibia, writing: "In present Namibia, the question of economic development takes a back seat to politics and in worse cases to history. In the minds of many government officials, the feelings of SWAPO politicians are generally regarded as important compared to the country's development plans and targets. In some cases, national development targets are superseded by short-term goals of politicians ranging from electioneering to pure corruption. Egoistic politicians prefer to hear the replay of their own historical narratives of their generational 'bravery' instead of serious questions of economic development, as we have seen with the countrywide protests and demands for land and housing. This serious matter of economic development was initially met with indifference and reference to history to remind the masses how bravely the heroes fought to bring 'peace and stability'."

Amupanda points out that such thinking is precisely why Deng Xiaoping was excommunicated by Mao. He explains that the lesson to learn from China is the urgency to "prioritise economic development above politics, heroism and sloganeering." Amupanda also notes that China decided to tweak socialism to match the realities of Chinese society, or what Xiaoping termed as "Socialism with Chinese characteristics." He contrasts this with SWAPO, which purported itself to be a socialist movement during the anti-colonial struggle, but after independence "followed the path of brutal neoliberal macroeconomic policies without due regard or whatsoever of Namibian context and characteristics."

There is also the problem of "indigenisation" which Amupanda references as well. Amupanda notes that the government reinforces and assists the "white economy" which is regarded as the Namibian economy. This strategy does not address the issue of economic redistribution in a society where Europeans, who make up 5 percent of the population, own more than 90 percent of the economy. This is not much different than the situation in South Africa following the end of apartheid.

In conclusion, I will state that the struggle in Namibia is not much different than the struggle in much of the rest of Africa. Namibia waged a struggle against colonialism. That struggle resulted in political independence, but little more than that. Economic struggles in Namibia have continued, especially regarding wealth inequality. The passing of Toivo ya Toivo is a cause to reflect on some of the shortcomings of the independence movement—shortcomings which have been clearly articulated by Amupanda, who has undertaken the struggle to challenge wealth inequality and the uneven distribution of land.

Selected References:

Denis Herbstein, "Andimba Toivo ya Toivo obituary," *The Guardian,* June 27, 2017.

Job Shipululo Amupanda, "Deng Xiaoping and the Chinese Developmental State: Lessons from Namibia," Strategic Review for Southern Africa, Vol 38, No 2, 2016.

7 THE POLITICAL DOUBLE-STANDARD IN NIGERIA

This is a short paper which addresses the problem of hypocritical leadership in Africa following reports that a Nigerian senator was caught having an extramarital affair in 2017.

When Bukar Abba Ibrahim served as the governor of Yobe State in Nigeria he implemented Sharia Law. Recently Ibrahim, who is now serving as a senator in Nigeria, was caught on video having an extramarital affair. Under Sharia Law a man is given one hundred lashes for committing adultery, but when Ibrahim was caught in the act—caught on video, I might add—the response from the senator was to announce that he was commencing an investigation to find out why the video of him was circulating.

Ibrahim also complained: "Is it because I am a public official then I am not supposed to be entitled to private life?" This is a rather astonishing claim from a public official who is willing to pass religious laws which govern the private lives of others, but he also wants to be free to violate those very laws in his own private conduct. The Islamic based Sharia Law apparently does not apply to Ibrahim. Also keep in mind that Ibrahim is already married to three women, which is permitted by Islamic law, but this is not enough for the senator. In fact, this was not even the first time that Senator Ibrahim was caught in such a scandal. The woman who submitted the video of Ibrahim getting dressed after committing the act did so for fear of her own life because Ibrahim had a previous affair with a high school girl who reportedly disappeared afterwards. One would assume that her disappearance was to keep the affair silent. The woman included her face in the video so that she can be identified in case she goes missing as well.

This scandal exposed some very basic problems in Nigeria's politics regarding corruption and immorality on the part of the political leadership, but the religious hypocrisy caught my attention especially. Throughout Africa it is not uncommon to find Christians or Muslims passing these religious based laws. For example, there are countries in Africa where homosexuality is an offense for which one can be imprisoned. The defense of such policies is that homosexuality is unnatural, immoral, violates religious laws, etc. These political leaders are so moral that homosexuality offends them, but theft, corruption, and misrule does not. These government ministers happily live in luxury as their people suffer in poverty.

In 2015, I read a story in the *Vanguard* which really conveyed the type of misery that Nigerian citizens are forced to live in. Folake Oduyoye gave birth to her fourth child. Due to complications she had to undergo surgery. Her husband did not have the money to pay the bill, so the hospital refused to discharge his wife. Folake Oduyoye developed more complications while she was in the hospital and the hospital refused to treat her. They also refused to discharge her so that she could get treatment elsewhere. She eventually died right there in the hospital because she was refused treatment. The same report noted that 144 Nigerian women die daily due to complications.

This is the type of misery that the people in Nigeria live in and there are politicians such as Ibrahim who see fit to pass harsh religious laws on the poor people of Nigeria which he himself does not even live by. But such is the state of politics in Nigeria.

8 AN EXCHANGE ON MARXISM-LENINISM

The following chapter is an email exchange between Tony Baker and Eddie Wilson on the topic of Marxism-Leninism in Africa.

Tony Baker: Good evening Eddie. We have been comrades for several years now and you are one of the most brilliant revolutionary minds that I know, but one thing that I have never understood is your opposition to Marxism-Leninism. You seem to understand the nature of class struggle that Africans around the world face and you are very critical of capitalism and imperialism, but I want to know why you reject Marxism-Leninism as the only practical ideological solution.

Eddie Wilson: Some African states turned to Marxism-Leninism. I think, in theory, Marxism is a great idea. It promises the creation of a society where there is no capitalist ruling class to dominate the workers and exploit their labor, so that the worker is able to earn all of the profits that are produced by his or her labor. The problem with Marxism is that Marx seemed to have assumed that the transition to this communist society was inevitable, but the communist revolution that Marx envisioned never happened. Marx believed that the communist revolution—which was a revolution in which the workers rise up and overthrow the ruling class—would take place in industrialized capitalist societies. Instead, the communist revolution that Marx envisioned took place in Russia, which at the time was not an industrialized capitalist state.

The communist state in Russia was not communist in the sense that Karl Marx envisioned, which is what I alluded to earlier. A violent and repressive one-party state was developed in Russia, and this was a one-party state that was controlled by a single dictator. This was not a nation ruled by the proletariat, but a nation run by a dictator. As we saw in the conflict between Joseph Stalin and Leon Trotsky, there were often even clashes for power and control between members of the Soviet ruling elite.

We find the Soviet Union engaging in the same type of imperialistic aggression that one would expect from capitalistic societies. The difference is that the Soviet aggression was launched against other European people, rather than colonizing Africa and Asia as other white people were doing. But it is very clear that at the time that Stalin took over, the revolutionary nature of the Soviet Union was finished, and Russia had effectively become a capitalist state run by a brutal dictatorship, rather than a state run by the working class.

Amos Wilson explained: "Study the hierarchy of the Russian Empire that rules over Poland and Yugoslavia and the nations of Eastern Europe." Wilson did not view the Soviets as being any different from any other group of white people who maintained imperialistic policies through the violence and suppression of others. He explains that the "Russian constitution is a most beautiful document, when you read it. And yet we see a minority of White Russians ruling over Moslems, other monitories, and other Europeans, despite what the constitution says."

I understand that the Marxist-Leninist position is to form a vanguard party and protect that party at all costs, even if doing so means curtailing liberties among the general populace—because such liberties are merely petty bourgeois rights anyway. I am not convinced by this position, however. I think this position lends itself to the very abuses that we eventually saw emerge in the Soviet Union.

I give the example of an individual named Jackie Creft, who was a member of the New Jewel Movement and part of the Grenadian government under Maurice Bishop—she was also the mother of Bishop's son. Creft ran into problems with the party because she was not a hardline Marxist. According to a Guyanese activist named Andaiye, Creft never spoke about Marx or Lenin. Creft also preferred to sit in the stands with the common people rather than being on stage with other party members. This seemed to have annoyed the party and she was censured for her lack of discipline.

I mention this because one of the issues with the Grenadian government was the hierarchical structure which seemed to be disconnected from the masses. Creft struggled with this within the party because she appeared to care more about the masses than the party's ideological attachment to Marxism-Leninism, or the formalities which come with being a member of the government. I think placing a vanguard party above the interests of the masses can lead to the type of issues which Grenada would later experience when the revolution collapsed. This is the same issue that we have seen with Marxism-Leninism throughout Africa as well.

The need to build and maintain the revolutionary vanguard party can lead to a type of dangerously rigid line of political thinking which can destabilize a party if certain members of that party are perceived to be too moderate in their Marxist views. This is what happened to Maurice Bishop in Grenada—he ended up being assassinated along with Creft. The same thing happened in Angola during the presidency of Agostinho Neto. Factionalism arose within the MPLA in Angola because Nito Alves and José Van Dúnem felt that Neto's policies were too moderate. They also criticized the heavy representation of white people and mulattos who were in the government. Both men were expelled from the Central Committee and later led an uprising which resulted in senior government leaders being killed. This is precisely what happened in Grenada, where certain elements of the ruling party came to believe that Maurice Bishop was simply too moderate.

The attempted coup also exposed some of the internal ideological differences among the Marxists themselves. Given that Angola professed Marxism-Leninism, Angola maintained a close relationship with the Soviet Union and with Cuba as well. Cuba and the Soviet Union had differing views on the situation in Angola, however. Cuba had assisted Neto in foiling the coup attempt, whereas the Soviet Union seemed to have favored Alves.

Overall, the Soviet Union did provide a great deal of support to Angola. The Soviet Union helped to arm the MPLA in their independence struggle against the Portuguese. After independence, the Soviet Union supported Angolan educational and training programs. Angolan students were also trained in the Soviet Union. Cuba provided similar support. This included providing military support by providing military training and stationing Cuban troops in Angola. Cuba also provided teachers and physicians who provided medical care for Angolans.

I am not suggesting that the Soviet Union did not do anything positive in terms of advancing Africa's development. My position is that Marxism-Leninism as an ideology has not been wholly successful in Africa. I can point to Angola to demonstrate this, but I would instead prefer to use Mozambique to illustrate my position. In Mozambique, the Mozambique Liberation Front (Frente de Libertação de Moçambique or FRELIMO) established a one-party state and adopted the ideology of Marxism-Leninism.

It is difficult to judge the true success of the Mozambique Liberation Front in the period following independence because Mozambique received its independence in 1975, and by 1977 a civil war broke out between the ruling government and the Mozambican National Resistance, which was an anti-communist organization that was supported by Rhodesia and South Africa. This war lasted until 1992 and what I want to note here is that before the war had finished, the Mozambique Liberation Front had abandoned communism. Joaquim Chissano took over control of the party when Samora Machel died, but he abandoned the ideology of Marxism-Leninism when it was becoming clear that the Soviet Union was losing the Cold War.

FRELIMO was formed in Tanzania in 1962 as an alliance of exiled political groups and began its armed struggle against Portuguese colonialism in 1964. There were internal struggles within the party itself. These struggles were often violent and led to the assassination of Eduardo Mondlane, who was the first president. His successor was Samora Machel, who stands out as being one of the most prominent African revolutionaries during this period of anti-colonial struggle in Africa. Under Machel's leadership, FRELIMO became a Marxist-Leninist organization. FRELIMO was also significantly influenced by China's experiences and by the ideas of Mao.

FRELIMO managed to defeat Portuguese colonialism and declare its independence. Under Machel's leadership, FRELIMO became a Marxist-Leninist political party. The discipline and integrity of Mozambique that was established under this new political direction is to be commended. Few party and government officials used their position to enrich themselves. Those who did were dismissed and occasionally executed. Mozambique had one of the lowest levels of corruption in Africa. I mention this to demonstrate that there were positive advances made by FRELIMO which should be recognized.

FRELIMO did face challenges, however. Independence was followed by 200,000 whites fleeing the country. This was a significant loss of skilled manpower, but Machel was undaunted in his attempt to transform Mozambique through nationalized plantations and businesses. Consistent with its Marxist-Leninist views, FRELIMO sought to reduce the influence of the Catholic Church by ordering an end to public religious festivals and taking over church property. This hostility extended to traditional religions as well. In 1977, Machel declared: "We affirm that our aim is to win total independence, to establish people's power, to build a new society without exploitation for the benefit of all those who consider themselves Mozambican."

Machel established himself as a respected revolutionary leader in Africa. After Machel died, Thomas Sankara described Machel as "a great friend of our revolution, a greater backer of our revolution." Indeed, the death of Machel was not only a blow to Mozambique, but a blow to the revolutionary struggle in Africa. Yet, there were already signs that socialism was weakening in Mozambique, even under Machel's leadership.

The government's policies failed to resolve the economic challenges that the nation was facing. FRELIMO debated whether to allow the peasantry to take back control of the land or to preserve the colonial infrastructure. FRELIMO opted for the latter and set up a state farm sector. The peasantry was also forced into collective villages, in a policy that was similar to a policy pursued by Julius Nyerere in Tanzania. These policies were not only an economic failure, but it alienated FRELIMO from much of the peasantry.

In "The Collapse of Mozambique Socialism," Dan O'Meara explains that in the 1980s the government of Mozambique was in a "contradictory process" and that "the major trend was towards increasing control and freezing out of large-scale (or indeed any form of) democratic participation both in economic decision-making and in the political life of the country." FRELIMO laid out a ten-year plan which projected a targeted annual economic growth rate of 14.7%. This rate was to be achieved through maximizing exports, which meant maximizing the agricultural production of the peasantry. President Machel declared that this objective was achievable because Mozambique had a vanguard party, but this goal was not achieved. Huge development projects brought Mozambique into debt to capitalist economies. This debt was more than double Mozambique's pre-independence Gross Domestic Product.

There were also political issues within FRELIMO itself as well. O'Meara explained: "During these years FRELIMO was a highly contradictory political movement. On the one hand, it was extremely centralized and commandist, moving slowly towards a growing personality cult around Samora Machel. On the other hand, it was at that stage still highly responsive to all kinds of mass pressures, and indeed organised wide-ranging consultative processes at all levels of society."

Aside from the economic struggles, Mozambique also faced destabilization attempts as well—not unlike the destabilization attempts that Angola faced with the South African and American supported UNITA rebel group. The Mozambican National Resistance (Resistência Nacional Moçambicana or RENAMO) was a rebel group which was supported by Rhodesia and South Africa for the purpose of overthrowing FRELIMO in Mozambique. The conflict between FRELIMO and RENAMO was a very destructive one. Not only did it drain the nation's economy, but RENAMO also directed its attacks against the civilian population.

In 1984, Mozambique signed a pact with South Africa, known as the Nkomati Accord. The war had such a devastating impact on Mozambique that FRELIMO had little option but to try to negotiate peace with South Africa. The accord was in a sense a compromise with FRELIMO's prior revolutionary position, but the pact with South Africa was not treated as such. O'Meara explained: "The incredulous party members and *cooperantes* who could not quite make this leap were bluntly told that anybody who said otherwise was an imperialist agent, a Trotskyist counterrevolutionary, a petty bourgeois defeatist and a myriad [of] other nasty things that no-one wanted to be. This was the first time such language was used in Mozambique and it sapped what was left of the critical spirit in the party and amongst the intelligentsia. It also destroyed what was left of the political credibility of FRELIMO."

Not only did the Nkomati Accord weaken FRELIMO ideologically and politically, but it did not even achieve what Mozambique had hoped. This compromise with South Africa followed with 800 ANC members being expelled from Mozambique. Meanwhile, South Africa secretly continued its support of RENAMO. The war was so devastating and destructive that over one million Mozambicans were killed by violence or starvation.

There were a lot of challenges confronting FRELIMO, but in the end the party opted to abandon Marxism-Leninism as the Cold War was coming to an end. Mengistu Haile Mariam of Ethiopia, José Eduardo dos Santos of Angola and Robert Mugabe of Zimbabwe also abandoned Marxism-Leninism at the end of the Cold War.

I don't think that many of the African political leaders that embraced Marxism were really trying to build a true communist society. What many of them were really doing was copying the Soviet model, which was a one-party state ruled by what was supposed to be a vanguard party. They were not truly working to create a state where workers were not being exploited and where there was common ownership of the means of production. Their ideological attachment was not to Marxism itself, but to the Soviet Union and when the Soviet Union fell, these political leaders had no choice but to adopt a new line of thinking.

So, these are some of the reasons I reject Marxism-Leninism as an ideology. I do not criticize others for taking this position, but in my view, I cannot see the practicality of this ideology. It failed in most of the African countries where it was applied, and it even failed in Russia. I understand your attachment to that ideology, but that is a particular ideology which I cannot share.

Tony Baker: I think you make the mistake of engaging in a bourgeois assessment. The fact that FRELIMO and other political parties in Africa abandoned Marxism-Leninism does not suggest that the idea itself was a failure or that it has no relevancy to the

African struggle. If we were to pursue that line of logic then you should have abandoned Pan-Africanism because of the failings of Marcus Garvey, but you seem to remain a devout follower of Garvey. Ideologies must be judged by their principles, not by the adherence of individuals to those principles.

You seem to have allowed yourself to be misguided by petit bourgeois Pan-Africanism, as opposed to the type of class based analysis which W.E.B. Du Bois' Pan-Africanism was rooted in. George Padmore created a great deal of confusion when he presented Pan-Africanism as an alternative to Communism. In doing so, he helped to move Pan-Africanists away from an understanding of the class nature of our struggle, and towards the utopian and reactionary vision of racial unity. Du Bois understood that we needed much more than racial unity. We needed unity of the working class masses of the world. This was a vision which was inspired by the Soviet Union.

Upon arriving in Russia, Du Bois observed: "Wild children were in the sewers of Moscow; food was scarce, clothes in rags, and the fear of renewed Western aggression hung like a pall. Yet Russia was and still is to my mind, the most hopeful land in the modern world. Never before had I seen a suppressed mass of poor, working people—people as ignorant, poor, superstitious and cowed as my own American Negroes—so lifted in hope and starry-eyed with new determination, as the peasants and workers of Russia, from Leningrad and Moscow to Gorki and from Kiev to Odessa; the art galleries were jammed, the theatres crowded, the schools opening to new places and new programs each day; and work was joy."

Your brand of Pan-Africanism, which is critical of the Soviet Union, is little more than the same petit bourgeois nationalism which was espoused by Garvey and by Padmore. It is not a Pan-Africanism which is rooted in the struggle of the masses and comes dangerously close to the type of liberal democracy which is often used to hide the truly imperialistic nature of capitalistic societies. This is what the revolutionary government of Maurice Bishop understood; free press and democratic elections are mere tools used by the bourgeoisie to lull the masses to sleep and to give them a false sense of freedom, while the means of production remain in the hands of a few.

What we need is a complete revolution, which means an overthrow of the ruling class. This can only be accomplished by workers of all racial backgrounds; not merely by the unification of African people only, which is what Pan-Africanists tend to only focus on. Once the ruling class has been overthrown, we need to maintain power after power has been seized. Bourgeois ideals of freedom of press and democracy—ideals espoused by the neo-liberal ruling class—are mere platitudes which serve as a disguise for the real intent of the ruling class, which is to maintain the status quo.

Societies which maintain a plurality of political parties only open themselves up to potential subversion from capitalistic forces which fund and support these opposition parties as fronts. Freedom of press opens up a revolutionary society to the possibility of counterrevolutionary propaganda. The United States has become the most advanced capitalist state in the world in part because it has fooled its citizenry with these same ideals.

Americans truly believe that they can vote for change. They believe in the "revolution" which Bernie Sanders preaches or in the dream of making America great again as Donald Trump purports. These notions of changing the society through using the methods given to the working class by the system is what ultimately perpetuates the system. It is what sustains the system, as it offers the illusion of change to the desperate masses who channel their energy towards chasing this illusion rather than towards chasing revolution. This is why we need to build vanguard political organizations, which are rooted in democratic centralism, as opposed to petty bourgeois politics.

The "imperialism" of the Soviet Union which you are denouncing was in fact an attempt to protect the revolutionary government from counterrevolutionary forces. These were the same forces which toppled Patrice Lumumba, Kwame Nkrumah, and Thomas Sankara. Revolutions must be protected at all costs, even if it means suppressing bourgeois rights and freedoms. Fidel Castro is perhaps the greatest example of this. The bourgeois press denounced him as a dictator and condemned the lack of freedoms in Cuba, but there was nothing that any of those powers could do to overthrow Castro or to destabilize his government. It is also no coincidence that Castro aligned himself with the Soviet Union. He understood that when he seized power, the Soviet Union at the time was a revolutionary force and that alignment with the Soviet Union was the only way for Castro to guard the gains that his revolution in Cuba was making. Therefore, your criticisms of what you refer to as imperialism and oppression in the Soviet Union are misguided. Those of us who are committed revolutionaries must not allow counterrevolutionary forces to manifest. Such forces must be crushed, and this cannot be done by using petit bourgeois liberalism.

Eddie Wilson's reply: The attempt to treat Garvey and Padmore as if they represent the same political ideology is misleading, since Padmore was one of Garvey's greatest detractors when Garvey was alive. Secondly, Garvey was also an admirer of Lenin. I think you are overstating the Pan-African hostility towards the Soviet Union. Garvey's fight was not a fight against the Soviet Union, neither was Malcolm's.

The reason why Padmore rejected communism is because he was frustrated with the fact that white communists were not as committed to the African struggle as he had hoped. Garvey had already perceived this, which is why he was critical of the communists in America. I acknowledged that the Soviet Union did in fact support revolutionary struggles in Africa, which should be commended, so do not read my criticisms of the Soviet Union as a dismissal of the support that Soviet Union provided for Africa's struggle against imperialism and Africa's development, although such support was clearly ideologically motivated to a significant degree.

The Pan-African position, as you know, is not one that is necessarily hostile to Marxism. I think it is necessary to strike a balance between class and race consciousness, but I simply do not see a solution to this issue in anything that the Soviet Union has presented. But above all else, I am looking for strategies and tactics which work for the advancement of African people. Unfortunately, it has been very difficult to find examples of where Marxism-Leninism has worked because it is very difficult to find examples where the leadership is interested in building societies which are free of class exploitation. In your response you offered the usual rhetorical points that I have become very familiar with, but we cannot advance a revolutionary struggle on theory alone.

We need examples. We need models.

Castro accomplished many great things while he was in power, but there were also things that were not addressed regarding racism in Cuba and the suppression of the African population. Marxism-Leninism focuses on class theory and class struggle, which has at times blinded its adherents to racial struggle. In some ways Castro also falls in line with the white communists who were not completely and totally committed to the liberation of African people. But that is really not the issue in contention here. What I intended to do was to demonstrate why it is I think Marxism-Leninism failed in Africa. It may have fared better in Cuba, but the African population in Cuba is still not completely liberated yet. Perhaps more important to the nature of this discussion is the fact that Cuba suffered several setbacks when the Soviet Union fell. These setbacks weakened Cuba's economy and I think a case can be made that Cuba may have been too closely aligned with the Soviet Union.

I want to be clear that I am not dismissing Marxism altogether and that I myself have been influenced to some degree by Marx's ideas. Walter Rodney wrote of "legal or armchair Marxists, who would like to see Marxism as merely another variant of philosophy and who treat it in a very eclectic fashion, as though one is free to draw from Marxism as one draws from Greek thought and its equivalent, without looking at the class base and without looking at whether an ideology is supportive of the status quo or not."

This is not what I am doing here. I understand very clearly the exploitative nature of capitalism and the Marxist theory of class struggle and class formations. My issue with what you are proposing is that I do not see it as a solution, and I have given examples for why I maintain this position. I do not share your view that ideas must be judged by their principles alone because plenty of ideas may work in theory, but application is always where the challenge is. I am not suggesting that the failures of Marxism-Leninism in Africa necessarily invalidates the idea or theory itself. It may very well be the theory which liberates African and it may very well be the case that Marxism-Leninism has yet to be properly applied in Africa, but as of right now one can only judge Marxism-Leninism in Africa by the results that it has produced, and I think that it is very telling that after the fall of the Soviet

Union so many African leaders abandoned Marxism-Leninism.

Tony Baker: Your reference to racism in Cuba under Castro is hardly surprising. One of the common smear tactics used by Pan-Africanists against Communism is to accuse white Communist figures of being racists. This has been done to Castro. This has also been done to Karl Marx as well. This is done by racial chauvinists who are not much better than white racists—chauvinists such as Elijah Muhammad, who would have had us believe that all white people are devils, when he enriched himself with reactionary religious dogma. This type of racial chauvinism must be rejected because it is contrary to the spirit of true revolutionary Pan-Africanism. This is the spirit expressed by Du Bois, who wrote: "I believed and still believe that Karl Marx was one of the greatest men of modern times and that he put his finger squarely upon our difficulties when he said that economic foundations, the way in which men earn their living, are the determining factors in the development of civilization, in literature, religion, and the basic pattern of culture. And this conviction I had to express or spiritually die."

I assert that the same is true of Castro and Lenin as well. The fact that they were white men does not discount their ideas or their accomplishments, although the capitalists would have black people shun white revolutionaries, but heap praise on black reactionaries. We must avoid falling for the racist trap of the ruling class.

It is not Pan-Africanism or Communism as Padmore suggested, but Pan-Africanism and Communism. Padmore did not understand this, nor did Garvey, so in my view they represent the same side of the petit bourgeois ideology that has become pervasive within the Pan-African movement and I am disappointed to realize how much of this ideology has influenced you as well, although I am not surprised because on numerous occasions you have been an apologist for the reactionary nationalism of the Nation of Islam.

I am surprised that you accuse me of engaging in theory without practice, when theory and praxis is one of the core principles of Marxism-Leninism. This is why I mention actual revolutions. Did Garvey ever manage to successfully liberate a single African nation? No. But Lenin led a successful revolution. Castro led one as well. The successes of the Bolshevik Revolution and the Cuban Revolution demonstrate the validity of the Marxist-Leninist theory, even if it may not have worked in Mozambique. Although, I will add that it failed in Mozambique because the capitalist powers would not have allowed it to prevail.

In truth, the Soviet Union was the only true international ally that African people had as they fought against the forces of racism and colonialism. Even you acknowledge the support that the Soviet Union offered to revolutionary struggles in Africa, which is more than the Chinese offered. The Chinese Communists, with their revisionist Maoist theory, preached Communist revolution, but in practice they sided with the imperialist forces. Remember that China supported the capitalist backed UNITA rebel forces in Angola. Apart from this, did China offer the same material support to the anti-colonial struggles in Africa that was offered by the Soviet Union?

We need to develop an anti-capitalist and anti-imperialist ideology. Pan-Africanism alone cannot offer this because it is too vague and too abstract. It is also very easily exploited by our class enemies who can easily use the promise of racial unity to mask their class interests. I contend that Marxism-Leninism is the only ideology that is suited for guiding the class struggle that must be fought by African people around the world in conjunction with all oppressed working people around the world. If there is a better approach or a better ideology, then please inform me of it. Otherwise, you are engaging in the bourgeois practice of offering a form of faux revolutionary rhetoric which lacks the real revolutionary substance of Marxism-Leninism.

Eddie Wilson: I recognize Du Bois' quote about Marx from his autobiography, *Dusk of Dawn*. In that book Du Bois also mentions that he did not consider himself to be a communist, despite his obvious respect for Marx. In that very book, Du Bois actually has much to criticize about communists. Of Russia, Du Bois wrote: "We may, with dogged persistency, declare that deliberate murder, organized destruction and brute force cannot in the end bring and preserve human culture; but we must admit that nothing that Russia has done in war and mass murder exceeds what has been done and is being done by the rest of the civilized world."

These were the very same concerns that I raised as well regarding the oppressive nature of Russian society under communist rule. Here Du Bois acknowledges that Russia was behaving no differently from other "civilized" nations, which is an obvious reference to the Western capitalist nations which opposed Russia's communism.

Du Bois is also very critical of how the American Communist Party handled the Scottsboro cases. He stated that the problem here was the dogma of the American Communist Party. As I am sure you are aware, this was a case in which black boys were accused of attacking two white prostitutes on a train. Du Bois accused the American Communist Party of "senseless interference," which hindered the case. Du Bois believed that the boys could have been freed in a couple of years without much fanfare or publicity, but the American Communist Party wanted to use the opportunity to foment revolution in the United States, but this backfired because the communists were so ignorant about race prejudice in the United States that they tried to arouse white workers in America by defending black people who were accused of attacking white women. They did not realize that the white working class would always side with white women—even prostitutes—who were allegedly attacked by black men, regardless of the actual facts of the situation. Du Bois concluded that their methods were tragically wrong. This was because the white communists in America did not understand the racial element. They were too blinded by their vision of class struggle in a racist society.

The issue with Castro is that, like many white communists, he did not understand the racial struggle. He believed that class struggle was the solution to ending racial inequality, but this position has its limits, as Du Bois demonstrated. I am not a racial chauvinist. In fact, I am opposed to the chauvinism of the communists who dismiss Pan-Africanism and Black Nationalism without properly understanding the nature of the racial struggle which African people have been engaged in.

Communist China adds an interesting dimension to this exchange. I agree with you that China should not have supported UNITA, but we have to acknowledge the fact that there were some Pan-African revolutionaries who looked to the revolution in China for inspiration. In his "Message to the Grassroots" speech Malcolm X presented China as an example of a revolution which wiped out the Uncle Toms. Malcolm referenced an article that he read in which a nine-year old Chinese girl killed her father because he was an "Uncle Tom Chinaman." Malcolm concluded by stating "today it's one of the toughest, roughest, most feared countries on this earth—by the white man. 'Cause there are no Uncle Toms over there."

Walter Rodney contrasted the Chinese population in the Caribbean with Mao's revolution in China: "The Chinese, on the other hand, are a former labouring group who have now become bastions of white West Indian social structure. The Chinese of the People's Republic of China have long broken with and are fighting against white imperialism, but our Chinese have nothing to do with that movement. They are to be identified with Chiang-Kai-Shek and not Chairman Mao Tse-tung." We also know that the Black Panther Party was heavily influenced by Mao. The Panthers went so far as to sell copies of Mao's book to raise funds. The Nigerian nationalist leader Funmilayo Kuti visited China where she met Mao.

China represented a non-white nation which had engaged in a communist revolution. For this reason, China attracted the support of Pan-Africanist revolutionaries, who were waging a struggle against white racism and capitalist exploitation. Indeed, I do think that there are aspects of the Chinese Revolution which African people can take lessons from, but I am not a Maoist largely because I think the ideological solutions to our problems should be rooted in African culture and history before anything else. If that makes me a chauvinist then so be it, but Karl Marx's theories were rooted in his own European society, not in African society. Does that make Marx a chauvinist for considering the interests of Europe before Africa?

As I stated, I do agree that it was a mistake for China to support the imperialist supported UNITA group in Angola, but I also think that the Soviet Union was equally as wrong for supporting the Derg in Ethiopia, which included providing military support so that Mengistu could put down revolts against his dictatorship. Cuba also supported the Derg and provided military support as well. As I stated before, the Soviet Union's support for revolutionary struggles in Africa was purely ideological. What the Soviet support for the Derg demonstrated was that the Soviet Union was willing to support counterrevolutionary leaders who professed Marxism-Leninism. Cuba, being closely aligned with the Soviet Union, went along with this counterrevolutionary policy of supporting the Derg.

The alternatives to Marxism-Leninism are there and have been there long before Marx and Lenin. Did the people of Haiti wait for the ideology of Marx and Lenin to liberate them? Did Nat Turner and Harriet Tubman know about Marx and Lenin before they rebelled against slavery?

I repeat a point that I made before, which is that I am not opposed to what Marxism-Leninism presents in theory, but in practice I do not see where it has worked in Africa. I think many of the African leaders were just imitating the Soviet Union's model and that model did not even work for the Soviet Union, which is why so many African leaders abandoned it. As someone who does not espouse that theory, it is not my duty to make that theory work for African people if it has failed several times in the past. That burden falls on you.

9 THE BLACK FAMILY AND SELF-LOVE

In this paper Eddie Wilson addressed the topic of the disintegration of the black family and proposes a solution that is based on revolutionary self-love and self-acceptance on the part of African Americans. This is followed by a published response from John Walks, leading to an exchange between the two. The exchange between the two is a continuation of the debate over African civilization versus Western civilization, which was discussed in **The Black African Crisis in the Age of a Black President.**

When the topic of the African American family comes up, we have those individuals who try to frame the issue as one of "traditional values." They say that African Americans are in the position that we are in because we lack traditional family values, but what are traditional family values? Whose values are we referring to? Are we referring to Eurocentric family values or of African family values? They never make this distinction, but I am prepared to make it here in this essay because what I have always been an advocate for is thinking outside of this Eurocentric framework that we are often trapped in. We need to expand our worldviews and start inquiring about how we operated as a people prior to our enslavement.

It is first necessary to dispel some myths. When we talk about poverty and crime in the African community, we are not talking about issues that stem from a lack of family values. Take Donald

Trump, for example. This is a man who is a billionaire, yet he did not achieve his financial success through having proper family values or good morals. He did not achieve his success through honesty, so if lack of family values and lack of proper morals made you poor then Donald Trump shouldn't be a billionaire. I do not think that the issue of poverty is necessarily an issue of morality for that reason.

We also have a tendency to judge African people from a particular moral standard in this society. The moral deficiencies among African people have been a serious focus of European people because our supposed moral deficiencies were a justification for our oppression. Africans were depicted as savages, cannibals, heathens, and the like. Therefore, if Africans were more civilized—if Africans were to simply accept Christ as our lord and savior—there would have been no need to enslave us or to colonize us. It was our own fault that we were enslaved because we not were not as civilized or as moral as Europeans. This is the type of justification which Europeans give.

These were the arguments put forward to justify oppressing us and it had very little to do with the lack of a black father in the household. So, it has often been these moral judgements that have been used to justify the oppression and mistreatment of African people, but what of the morality of white people? What of the morality of the very people who oppressed and enslaved us?

I mentioned Trump because Trump is actually the quintessential representation of America's capitalist morals. This is a man that values wealth and power. Everything for him is connected to his wealth, which is why he once sued someone for referring to him as a millionaire rather than a billionaire. These are the types of values that capitalism is built on. This society—American society—is one that was built on the premise that the profits from slavery were of more value than the human beings that were being enslaved. Our motto in America is essentially "profits over people." And as a result of this, relationships that occur within the context of this very materialistic society tend to be superficial relationships. So, it is simply hypocritical to me that a society which would elect Donald Trump as president would preach moral values as if moral values is why a man like Trump is successful.

One of the reasons why I am suspicious of people who speak of problems within the African community as an issue of values is that it lacks historical perspective. What I mean by this is that lack of values is not why we were enslaved. It's not why we were colonized. Those things happened to us because the people that oppressed us lacked values. They lacked morals or compassion, but in order to justify their colonization of African people, Europeans portrayed us as being savage. Cecil Rhodes massacred thousands of African people, but he explained: "I contend that we are the finest race in the world and that the more of the world we inhabit the better it is for the human race." Western imperialism was often justified under the pretext of bettering humanity and spreading civilization to a morally inferior people.

We must break away from this notion that a lack of values and morals are the root of our problem. The root of our problem is that we are a colonized people, and if you don't believe that then ask yourself what kind of names do you wear? My name is Wilson. That's not an African name. That's the name of some European slave master that owned my ancestors. That was a name that was imposed on me. The colonizer always seeks to impose his culture and identity on the colonized as an aspect of that colonial domination because if you accept my worldview and you think like me then you will never rebel against me, or if you do rebel you will ultimately end up fighting yourself because you cannot separate yourself from your colonial masters. This is what we have seen all over Africa since independence. The minds of our people in Africa have been so colonized that we have taken over power from our former colonizers and then turned around and served their agenda. Leon M'ba, who was the president of Gabon, was known to have said that all Gabonese have two fatherlands, Gabon and France. We are so colonized that we cannot tell ourselves apart from the people that have colonized us, and as a result we think that their interests are our interests when the reality is that they have a vested interest in our continued oppression and colonization. A *New York Times* report from 1964 described M'ba, who had recently been overthrown, as "one of France's best friends in Africa." ("Man in the News; Ousted Gabonese," *New York Times*, Feb. 19, 1964).

Now that I have dealt with the myth that moral and financial success in America are intertwined, we will have to address the question of how do we go about addressing the issues that impact the black family. When we arrived on the shores of the United States we were stripped of our languages and customs, which included family customs. Families were broken up and parents were separated from their children. This was the first traumatic blow that the black family structure experienced. Since we have been in the United States it has always been a challenge to hold together the black family structure in the face of not only families being split up, but of fathers being murdered. For those of you that have read Malcolm X's autobiography, recall that his family was split up after his father was murdered by racists and his mother suffered a mental breakdown. Think about how many families were broken up because the father was lynched.

Also keep in mind that historically, the black family unit has been under tremendous strain within this American system. We see this even within the modern context of mass incarceration and the killing of black men, either by the police or by other black men. We are in a situation still where black men are constantly being removed from their families by violence. Of course, we have brothers that walk away under their own free will as well or produce children that they have no intent on raising. The point is to be made that the black family is under strain from several sources which are political, economic, and cultural. How do we address all of these issues which constrict and hinder the development of true love and self-acceptance among African people?

We lost our original family models and came to a society which has been very hostile towards the black family. This is a society that has done so much to break up the family unit that we had, and as I explained before, we live in a society in which the relationships that are formed tend to be very superficial, so it is difficult to build and sustain a healthy family structure in the type of society in which we live.

We must realize that boys must be taught how to be men. Girls must be taught how to be women. This is not something that just happens biologically as children mature. And what we also must realize is that as children grow into adulthood they must be taught how to relate to members of the other sex. A marriage needs a proper foundation. It is not enough simply to say that you love someone and wish to marry for that reason. What is that love based on? This is why I stress the fact that both parties in the marriage need to have certain shared goals and shared motivations. There must also be shared expectations as well. If you go into a marriage simply because you love the other person and simply because they make you feel good, then you are not going into a marriage with a proper foundation. What happens when those good feelings go away? We hear often about marriages that fall apart because one person in the relationship falls out of love with the other person. That's because feelings are fleeting things and for that reason, we cannot define love as being merely a good feeling because good feelings are not perpetual. The bliss that newlyweds feel is not a permanent state. What happens when a marriage is no longer new or exciting? Many of us do not think about this or prepare for this.

So many of us get into relationships for the wrong reasons. Sometimes relations are driven by the fear of being alone. Often, we have very selfish reasons for being in relationships. We run into these relationships to mask our own insecurities and to bury those insecurities in another person. We act as though the other person in the relationship exists to please us and to make us happy. The other person then becomes almost like an object or a tool for us. We use the other person in the same way one uses drugs or alcohol to escape from a problem or to cope. Sometimes these relationships actually make the problem worse, just like substance abuse can make an emotional problem worse.

You can certainly be fulfilled and happy in a relationship, but do not make the mistake of thinking that a relationship will give you fulfillment and happiness where it is lacking. You cannot be an incomplete human being and be in a healthy and productive relationship, yet too many people get into these relationships looking for a soulmate or looking for someone that they think will complete them. Many of us even make the mistake of thinking that our love of a person can somehow change them. We have all these romantic notions of love which makes us think that merely being in love transforms you or it transforms the person that you love, but it doesn't work that way. Healthy relationships must be built on healthy and strong foundations.

To create stable and proper relationships we therefore must build proper foundations. I will start by discussing our black boys and how they are prepared for manhood. How are these boys raised to feel about black women? What messages does society teach them about black women or about themselves? Very often our boys grow up and learn to relate to women in very negative ways. Being a man to them is not the ability to care for a woman or to provide for a woman. It is not your ability to respect women. Manhood for them is the ability to use women. It is their ability to exploit women to enhance their ego or their perceived status. These are not men who are looking for partners that they can build with. They are looking for a quick thrill or for some quick pleasure, but they are not looking to build anything meaningful. They are not looking to build something that can be passed down to future generations.

So, what we must do is reeducate these men to respect their women. This was a value that was very traditionally African. The Kouroukan Fouga was the constitution of the Mali Empire and one of the provisions of this constitution stated, very plainly: "Never offend women, our mothers." Respect for women was written into law in Mali. In a society with values such as this you did not find men calling women out of their names. In truth, in many African societies a man prostrated to their mother and other senior female relatives. In societies of such nature, you simply have a different type of social interaction between men and women, which leads to a different type of family unit.

Regarding family structures, we also must be very conscious about how we are raising our children to perceive themselves and to perceive other people. We must ensure that our children are raised with positive conceptions of themselves and their identities so that they have a very strong foundation to build on. When you are raising a child, you must be cautious of the fact that you are not just raising a child. You are raising someone's future husband or future wife. You are raising a future father or a future mother. You are not raising children, but rather you are raising adults and how you raise them will have an impact on not only that child, but the people around that child. This is why in African societies a marriage was not a marriage between a man and a woman, but a marriage between two families because we understood that raising a child was a community effort. The reason for this is because a child that is not properly trained for adulthood becomes a problem to the very community that he or she lives in. Asa G. Hilliard wrote: "Undereducated or uneducated Americans will become a burden on the society." ("From Hurdles to Standards of Quality in Teacher Testing", *The Journal of Negro Education*, Vol. 55, No. 3, 1986). Not only will these people become a burden on the society, but they could even destroy the society.

Uneducated Africans have been a tremendous burden to us, and we must fix this issue with proper African-centered education that stresses self-love and self-fulfillment. We must provide the sort of education that allows our children to properly understand and confront the challenges that face them because too often we have seen our people develop self-destructive behaviors and tendencies in response to oppression. The anger that these young men feel may be justified, but it is not channeled properly. For example, when African men are oppressed, we have a very silly habit of turning against each other and turning against our women. Those rebels in the Congo, rather than waging war against the neo-colonial forces that run the Congo, target innocent and defenseless women and children. Look at Guinea. In 2008 there was a coup in Guinea, which was led by Moussa Dadis Camara. Camara established one of many brutal military regimes that we have seen across Africa. In 2009 this regime killed over 100 protestors during a demonstration against the government. Under Camara's rule, soldiers were also known to have engaged in robberies and rape. Camara was eventually forced into exile after he was ousted from power. ("Guinea stadium massacre: Former ruler Camara indicted," *BBC*, July 9, 2015).

Soldiers and rebels in Africa are often not well-trained. They are merely confused and angry men who are given some weapons and told to go out and cause havoc. "Go rape and kill." Many of our young men in the States have the same mentality. They pick up a gun and then use that gun to harm their own people and end up harming themselves as well. As I stated, the anger and frustration are justified. The violent African rebel groups and the violent American gangs are partly driven by the desire to survive in a hostile environment which does not offer much love, guidance, and opportunities for success, so they engage in behaviors which destroy the society and destroy themselves in the process because they have not been truly educated to understand how to properly confront these challenges.

The solution to this is, as I noted, developing an African-centered education for our children that will truly empower them in the face of the struggles that we face. When we look at African culture, we do find models for training children and preparing them for adulthood. I will offer a specific example of a manhood initiation ritual in Africa. Those of you that have read Nelson Mandela's autobiography are perhaps familiar with much of what I have said thus far because Mandela details a lot of these traditions. Mandela writes in his book that when he was sixteen, he underwent this ritual. In Xhosa society a boy becomes a man through the tradition of circumcision. Mandela writes about being taken into a secluded valley with other boys. Mandela writes: "I was tense and anxious, uncertain of how I would react when the critical moment came. Flinching or crying out was a sign of weakness and stigmatized one's manhood. I was determined not to disgrace myself, the group, or my guardian. Circumcision is a trial of bravery and stoicism; no anesthetic is used; a man must suffer in silence."

What he was describing here was that this was not only a ritual in which boys were now considered men, but a ritual in which the young men involved were learning about certain expectations that Xhosa society placed on a man. A man was supposed to be brave in the face of pain. Moreover, in being brave and being strong the man was not only representing himself, but his group. After being circumcised, a guardian explained to the young men the rules that they were to follow to enter manhood properly.

This was a society where young men were initiated into manhood and trained for manhood. Similar customs were put in place for women as well. We must realize that boys must be taught how to be men. Girls must be taught how to be women. This is not something that just happens biologically as children mature. As children grow into adulthood they must be taught how to relate to members of the other sex. A marriage needs a proper foundation. It is not enough simply to say that you love someone and want to marry that person for that reason. What is that love based on? This is why I stress the fact that both parties in the marriage need to have certain shared goals and shared motivations. There must also be shared expectations as well.

We are often sold this concept of romantic love. You meet

someone, the two of you fall in love, and you get married. But as a community, we have to start defining love in a way that is not only emotional or romantic, but in a way that is also real and practical. Love for us cannot be a matter of how you feel, but what you do. I can say "I love you" all I want, but it is meaningless if my words are not supported by actions. We must then define what these actions are. How do two people who are in love behave?

It is perhaps worth noting that the concept of romantic love as we think of it in Western society is in fact alien to African societies. One of the areas where Africans and Europeans clashed was that Europeans disapproved of certain aspects of Africa's marital customs, such as arranged marriages and polygamy. This seemed contrary to the European view of marriage, which, at that particular time, was a view that marriage is a union between two individuals who develop a strong affection for each other and marry on the basis of this affection, but affection alone is not enough.

I want to mention Mandela again in this context. Mandela's life is also relevant for discussion here because he mentions in his autobiography that one of the factors that led to the end of his first marriage to a woman named Evelyn was that she assumed that at some point he would have given up on politics. During the marriage, Evelyn became a Jehovah's Witness. Mandela tried to persuade her of the necessity of the struggle, while she attempted to persuade him of the value of religious faith. Mandela explained that Evelyn's "faith taught passivity and submissiveness in the face of oppression, something I could not accept."

This conflict between politics and religion also created tension over how to raise the children. Mandela wanted to raise them to be interested in politics and Evelyn wanted them to be religious. Evelyn made Mandela choose between his work with the African National Congress or their marriage. He was unable to give up the political struggle and this became an irreconcilable difference, which contributed to the end of his first marriage.

They were unable to come to a compromise and the marriage ended. Now, Mandela mentions earlier in his autobiography that the two "fell in love." This is what I mean when I say we must define love. The love that Mandela had for Evelyn was not a love rooted in a shared vision between the two, so the relationship ended. Of course, having a normal family life was something that Mandela had to sacrifice as part of the struggle that he was engaged in, and this was his biggest regret, but I mentioned Mandela's first marriage because it is a typical example of how love alone is not enough to sustain a marriage, especially if the people involved do not have shared interests.

This is particularly relevant when we talk about the black family and having a revolutionary type of love which can advance us collectively as a people. This is the type of love that has to exist within the context of a shared political struggle for our collective liberation and advancement. This is why marriage has to be a political act, a deliberate political act which seeks to advance our collective interests. Marriages cannot be built on sentiment alone.

Marriage is political. It is a politically recognized union. This is what the whole struggle for marriage equality in America was about; getting the American government to legally recognize homosexual unions. What I am suggesting is that black people must recognize this and be deliberate in our decision to form political unions.

I am not suggesting that this needs to be the only consideration, but I mention Mandela here because I am sure most people would agree—or should agree—with Mandela that the political struggle is more important than an apolitical religious approach, yet that distinction is what ended his first marriage. Therefore, when we talk about forming family unions, how do we do so in such a way where both partners understand the importance of commitment to the larger struggle. Revolutionary love is the love between two people who understand that it is their duty to transform society.

This means that you can have your individual preferences in a marriage, but at what point do we enter into marriages with the common goal or common vision of black empowerment and black liberation. That is what I want us to start thinking about. We must see marriage not merely as a union of two individuals, but a union of a common vision or a common purpose. It is a political union of individuals who are committed to change and liberation.

Keep in mind that when I speak of the black family, I am speaking about a revolutionary black family. I am speaking about a black family unit that comes together to resist racism and all other forms of oppression against African people. I would even argue that black love—real black love—is a revolutionary act in a society that teaches black people to hate themselves and to hate each other. And real love is a revolutionary act in a superficial society that does not promote such love.

This is also why studying our African culture is important because this was a very family-centered culture. In African culture you did not marry an individual, but you married into a family. Very often the customs of these societies dictated that if a man wanted to marry a woman, he had to win the favor of her family. African marital customs were very diverse and I do not intend to discuss the various martial traditions in African this piece, but the point that is to be made here is that as African people we had our own cultural definitions of marriage and, as I would argue, those definitions are much needed given the present issues that we face. As I noted before, the concept of romantic love in Western society was not quite the concept of marriage that we had in Africa. I am not suggesting that one is necessarily morally superior to the other, but I think we should at least study and understand the African models that we had prior to colonialism because there are elements to the African society which I believe will serve us practically as we address some of the issues that confront us.

The goal is self-acceptance, self-love, and self-transformation as a people; or what Abraham Maslow would refer to as "self-actualization." We ultimately cannot achieve this as African people within a society that oppresses us, so it becomes necessary to rebel against the injustices that are inflicted on us. It is through this act of rebellion against injustice that many of us will come to find our manhood and our womanhood—to self-actualize. It is through this act of rebellion that we will accept ourselves and love ourselves, while also loving each other in the process. Self-love implies a love for the community and a love for the community implies self-love. You cannot fully and completely experience one without the other.

An African who is filled with self-love and filled with love for his or her people cannot enrich himself or herself by damaging his or her own community. You must understand that when you adopt the values of this consumer society, you adopt values that are materialistic, shallow, and ultimately destructive to ourselves, and even destructive to those around you. You fight and kill each other over a pair of shoes because they have some basketball player's name on it. You will fight and kill each other over a car because you saw that car being advertised on the television or on the computer screen. This is what this culture does to our people.

When you are filled with self-hatred and hatred towards African people, you will then come to value money and material items over your people and will do whatever it takes to get that money and get those items, even if it means harming your own people to get those items. You have to understand that crime in our communities is not fueled by the fact that we lack traditional American values. It is fueled because we have embraced traditional American values, which are values based on acquiring wealth, even if it means harming your own community to acquire that wealth.

When you are filled with self-hatred and hatred towards African people, you come to embrace a very destructive type of individualism. This notion of individualism is something that we have to confront as well. We are at once unique individuals, yet also the products of the culture or society which we come from. Take for example someone like Adolf Hitler. There is little question among most people that what Hitler and the Nazis did was evil, but Hitler himself was the product of a Western society which was built on racism, violence, and conquest. At the time of Hitler's emergence Germany had lost its African colonies as a result of losing the First World War, but prior to that Germany was no different from the other European nations which were building their wealth through the exploitation of African people. The foundations for Hitler's vision of racial superiority were deeply entrenched in Germany and in Western culture long before Hitler was born, so we cannot look at Hitler merely as an evil individual. We must view him as a product of an imperialistic and racist society. Even his views on Jewish people were deeply rooted in Europe's own history of anti-Jewish prejudice.

We are often given this view that Hitler was someone who was uniquely evil in history, but he was very much a product of the society which he was raised in. Likewise, many of us are products of the society which we are raised in. We are raised in societies which hate African people, so we come to hate ourselves and our people. We are raised in selfish and individualistic societies, so we internalize these values. We became selfish and individualistic.

So, if we are serious about addressing this issue within the black family—which is really an issue between black men and black women—then we have to redefine ourselves in a positive manner. We have to raise children that not only have a positive sense of self, but also grow up having a constructive understanding of love.

John Walks' reply: Eddie Wilson once again offers a romanticized view of Africa as a practical solution to the real problems that black Americans face. As is typical of Pan-African romanticizers such as Wilson, everything is the fault of the white man. Black Americans have unstable family lives because of slavery; because the white man took away the culture of black Americans. According to his version of history, Africa was a paradise before the white man. Everyone was united and there were no familial problems or broken homes. It is because he sees Africa as a paradise that Wilson presents the solution to the problem as merely returning to some idyllic period in the African past.

Wilson sees no value in Western values and morals, but he certainly finds values and morals in African culture, even in places where none exist. In Wilson's narrative of Africa, circumcision rituals are a model for manhood initiation. Causing pain and suffering to young boys is, in Wilson's mind, all a part of teaching young boys to become great men. Why not? It certainly worked for Nelson Mandela after all. Would Wilson advocate the same thing for African women? Is female circumcision (otherwise known as female genital mutilation) also a treasured African tradition which helps young girls to understand what it is to be a woman? Or do we just ignore that particular African tradition because it does not fit the very selective narrative that Mr. Wilson is trying to portray?

In Wilson's romanticized version of history, the Mali Empire is presented as a model for respect for women. Wilson cites article 14 of Mali's constitution to make this point, but he dares not inform readers that the very next article reads: "Never beat a married woman before her husband has tried to correct the problem." That's right! The people of Mali respected women so much that beating married women was allowed in Mali's constitution. Are these the type of traditional African family values that Wilson is advocating for? Perhaps Wilson is familiar with the works of Mungo Park, who observed that whenever the wives of African men would quarrel with each other—polygamy was also part of the great family morals of traditional African society which Wilson advocates—then "the husband decides between them; and sometimes finds it necessary to administer a little corporal chastisement," before tranquility between the wives can be restored. Wife beating is a part of African culture, but Wilson does not speak of this because it ruins his romantic view of family life in Africa. Wilson seems to envision marriage as being an affection-less and emotionless affair, which is not surprising because he promotes societies in which beating one's wife and taking many wives were permitted.

The fact of the matter is that family values are a significant part of what is wrong with African American culture. This is not a racist statement, but a factual one. A child raised in a single-parent household is less likely to succeed, and this is also true of white families as well. Wilson acknowledges that this is a problem, but he advocates for a very strange concept of "revolutionary" love because he believes that there is some kind of conspiracy to destroy the black family on the part of white people. The truth is that white people themselves are now struggling to maintain a healthy family structure. The Judeo-Christian values which Western civilization is built on is crumbling and needs to be repaired. The answer is not in some mystical and utopian African past, which is rooted more so in Wilson's imagination than in actual reality.

Wilson knows very well that Hitler was a perversion of Western values, so it is disingenuous for him to suggest that the Nazis are a standard by which Western civilization should be judged, especially since it was Western democracy which defeated Nazism. But in Mr. Wilson's racist world view, all white people are equally as bad and equally as evil. He leaves no room for nuance where white people are concerned.

I can safely say as a black man—one who does not have the racial prejudices that Mr. Wilson seems to possess—Western civilization is the greatest civilization that humanity has ever known and my concern is that we are losing the morality and the Judeo-Christian values which made the West great.

The irony is that even Wilson is aware of this, which is why he cites a Western psychologist named Abraham Maslow. The field of psychology itself is a Western tradition, so Wilson tries to demonize the West while also trying to pick and choose which aspects of the West he thinks are suitable for him. Frankly, this is disingenuous and only further contributes to the problem. It is time that we black people stopped blaming the white man and learned to become valuable members of the Western society in which we live.

Eddie Wilson responds: There's a video of Malcolm X being interviewed in public and the interviewer asked if anyone in the crowd would like to comment after hearing what Malcolm said. Up came a black man who explained that he did not agree with Malcolm and stated that all people have been mistreated. He continued to explain that "Negros" feel sorry for themselves and this sorrow, in his opinion, is what kept African Americans back.

Malcolm responded by pointing out that whenever "compromising Negroes" such as Martin Luther King spoke, no one in the press tried to counter what he says, but whenever a black man such as Malcolm says anything that white people don't like, the white man runs around to find some other black person to offset what was just said. This is the function that you serve, and I say this very respectfully. You seem to serve the role of countering whatever it is that I say, although I must admit that I was very surprised by your response because you actually made some attempt to engage in historical research before responding to me. In the last exchange that we had several years ago when I was interviewed on your show, I did point out the fact that your understanding of African history was very shallow, so I admire that you made the attempt to do some research here, but it is not enough.

Unfortunately, there is still some bias in your response, which I will address here. I have never suggested that Africa was a paradise before Europeans arrived. Far from it. My position is that there were many exemplary elements of African civilization, but all societies, just like individuals, must constantly strive to be improved. Let me address some of the points that you have raised.

I mentioned circumcision here because of what Nelson Mandela wrote in his autobiography. That should not be taken to necessarily be an endorsement of the practice, which is cruel in some respects. Nevertheless, it did serve an important societal function. It is also true that in African societies female circumcision was a ritual practice as well. It is not that I was ignoring it, but it really was not important to the main purpose of my article. I do not view African society as being stagnant and I do think that there are some traditions which are archaic and should be removed. Female circumcision is certainly one of those practices, and perhaps male circumcision as well.

You mentioned Judeo-Christian values but do keep in mind that the Hebrew people practiced both polygamy and circumcision, so such practices are within the cultural practices of Judeo-Christian society. Even the Bible would tell you that "wise" King Solomon had 700 wives, so polygamy is also a part of the Judeo-Christian tradition as well.

The main focus of my response is what you said regarding Mali because it demonstrates your lack of nuance in understanding these issues, historically. I do not advocate wife beating, nor is that why I made mention of Mali's constitution—which is known as the Kouroukan Fouga. I mentioned the Kouroukan Fouga to demonstrate that Mali was a society where respect for women was enshrined in law. Article 16 of that constitution stated: "Women, apart from their everyday occupations, should be associated with all our managements." This was not a society in which women were excluded, whereas in the United States, for a long time, women were not allowed the right to vote.

As I said, I do not defend or condone beating a woman, but let us place this in some sort of historical context. You quoted Mungo Park, who made reference to "a little corporal chastisement" and I would like to focus on the word little in that quote because he was in fact referring to a very light form of corporal punishment. Park explained that "if any one of the ladies complains to the chief of the town, that her husband has unjustly punished her, and shewn an undue partiality to some other of his wives, the affair is brought to a public trial." Therefore, women in Malian society were not completely without redress if her husband became too overbearing in his punishment of his wife. It is not as though a husband had free reign to mistreat his wife however he saw fit, which is why the constitution of Mali urged respect for women. Pre-colonial African society was not perfect, but it does not need to be perfect for us to draw ideas from. I certainly think that our African roots provide a strong foundation for us to build on.

It is true that I referred to Maslow, but this was because I do think that his concept of self-actualization is useful. African civilization has historically been very open and receptive to ideas which originate from the outside. The Romans killed Jesus and persecuted Christians, but the early Christians found safety and refuge in Africa. When the Prophet Muhammad began his teachings, he and his followers were persecuted in Mecca. The Prophet sent his followers to Ethiopia where he knew they would receive protection. So, there is no inconsistency on my part as a Pan-Africanist to adopt ideas of Western thinkers if those ideas can be practically applied to the African situation.

Europeans have done the same thing. You keep referring to a Judeo-Christian belief system which originated outside of Europe. Abraham, Moses, and Jesus were not Westerners. As Malcolm X once pointed out, there is not a single prophet in the Bible who came from Europe. In fact, African people could more rightfully lay claim to the Judeo-Christian traditional system of values than Europeans can because of the clear African influence on the Biblical religion of Abraham. Therefore, the very values which you espouse existed in Africa long before Europeans embraced them.

John Walks: I see you resort to quoting your favorite black racist, Malcolm X. The difference is that whereas Malcolm later abandoned his racism and hatred of white people, you bitterly hold on to your racism. This racism is sadly apparent by the manner in which you denigrated Martin Luther King in your reply. King was a proud Christian man who believed in America, but you seem to have an issue with black people who dare to believe in this great nation. I am surprised that your hatred of proud Christian Americans has not led you to denigrate Harriet Tubman and other proud black Christians in such a manner.

Nevertheless, your attempts at moral relativity are laughable. You are now trying to defend wife beating in Africa by suggesting that it was not so bad because if husbands went too far, the victims could seek redress. Your racial pride has reduced you to defending wife beating because you so strongly hold on to this view that Africans were all innocent victims of the vicious white man. At the same time, your moral relativity does not allow you to understand the important moral advancements which have been made by Western civilizations over the years.

I may not have your knowledge of Africa's history, but I do recognize racism when I see it and you are a Pan-African racist who detests Christianity and Western civilization, yet what you fail to realize is that the Pan-African message which you preach is based on upholding civilizations which engaged in polygamy, wife beating, human sacrifice, and tribal warfare. African culture was a primitive culture, but we have been fortunate enough to have been born in the most morally advanced nation in the history of the world. That nation is the United States.

The United States' morality is built on Christian morals, but you seem to think that America's morals are the reason why African American families are in disarray. This is a very incorrect position to hold. We should be encouraging Americans of all racial backgrounds to practice proper family values without trying to racialize the challenges that the American families confront.

Finally, how long will you hold on to this victim mentality and try to portray African Americans as victims of America. Americans abolished slavery and abolished Jim Crow. You pretend to be a historian, so I am sure you recognize the progress that America has made as a nation where the issue of race is concerned. Why do you seek division by ignoring how far we have come as a nation?

Eddie Wilson: I see that we have moved away from the topic of circumcision. Let me clarify my position as a Pan-Africanist. Not for you John because I have dealt with you enough to know that you are not interested in clarity. You much rather misrepresent my positions, but I wish to clarify for anyone who is reading this exchange.

The fact that I do not denigrate Harriet Tubman should be proof to anyone that I do not have any hatred for Christianity or people who practice that religion. My reference to Malcolm was not meant to denigrate King. I have a great deal of respect for King, but the fact is that King was someone who was more moderate and compromising than Malcolm was, so America was a bit more comfortable with King. I say a bit more comfortable because King suffered a great deal for his activism—more so than Malcolm did actually. This great "moral" nation which John is referring to is the very nation which inflicted this suffering on King because King dared to preach brotherhood and love.

I do not denigrate Tubman at all because she was one of the best examples of an African who struggled and fought to liberate her people in the United States. Tubman was also a victim of America's supposed morality. We obviously know that Tubman was born into slavery, and she had to liberate herself and her family from slavery, so I will not get into that discussion. Instead, let's discuss what happened to Harriet Tubman after slavery was abolished.

In 1865, after the end of the Civil War, which Tubman fought in, she attempted to travel from Philadelphia to New York on a train when a conductor removed her from a car. The conductor looked at her ticket and told Tubman that he didn't carry "niggers." When Tubman attempted to explain that she was employed by the government and was entitled to transportation, she was grabbed by her arm and forced out. Tubman was handled so violently that her arm was severely injured and had to be placed in a sling. This was how a veteran of the Civil War was being treated in the North. Women in Mali were treated with more dignity and respect than what was shown to Harriet Tubman, so that alone should be enough to destroy any notion that Western civilization was more morally advanced than African civilization was.

I have already stated that there was a time when women in America could not vote. In an interview which Eusi Kwayana conducted with a Guyanese organization known as Cuffy 250, Eusi explained the development of the village movement in Guyana. Coming out of slavery, Africans pooled together their resources and bought land. Africans then used this land to establish their own villages, the first of which was known as Victoria. Why do I mention this? I mention it because Africans established their own system of governance to manage this village. As Eusi Kwayana explained in the interview, the village held elections. Women in British Guiana, just as women in Britain and the United States, could not vote. In Victoria, however, there were no restrictions against women being able to vote. This was an internal government which was established by African people who were practicing African values, not the values of their European colonial masters. This is why I stress the fact that African culture was a culture which was generally very respectful of women and gave women a level of power and influence which simply did not exist in Western societies.

This respect for women formed the basis of Cheikh Anta Diop's argument regarding the cultural unity of Africa. In the fifteenth chapter of *Africa Must Unite*, Kwame Nkrumah begins by noting that there are obstacles in the way of African unity. One of these obstacles is lack of a common culture. Despite the vast cultural differences, Nkrumah also explained: "I am constantly impressed by how much we have in common. It is not just our colonial past, or the fact that we have aims in common, it is something which goes far deeper. I can best describe it as a sense of one-ness in that we are *Africans*."

Nkrumah was confronted with the challenge of finding a common cultural basis upon which African unity could be built. Cheikh Anta Diop was also confronting this same question, but he worked to resolve this question by looking at Africa's history to find some commonality among the various diverse cultures of Africa. In *The Cultural Unity of Black Africa*, Diop proposed that black people in Africa shared a common culture which originated from a single source: the Nile Valley. In "The Queenmother, Matriarchy, and the Question of Female Political Authority in Precolonial West African Monarchy", Tarikhu Farrar explained that Diop "viewed what he considered to be matriarchal family forms in Africa as an outgrowth of matrilineal descent systems. Moreover, he explained the generally higher status of women in ancient and later precolonial Africa (in comparison to Europe and Asia during the same period) in this light. His consideration of female political power in early Africa was connected to what, in his view, was an underlying matriarchal foundation."

Farrar challenges Diop's position that African culture stems from a single source. Farrar writes that Africa has been historically composed of "*relatively* distinct communities of culture, which, over the centuries, have not existed in isolation, but have interacted with one another, sharing elements of culture between them."

Diop was basing this view of cultural unity on the matrilineal nature of African societies in contrast to the patrilineal nature of European and Asian societies. I do not think that this approach goes deep enough in trying to establish a basis for cultural unity among African people, however. Diop was attempting to establish the centrality of the Nile Valley to the development of African culture, much in the same way that Greece is seen as being central to the development of Western civilization. As such, Diop's work is hindered by the fact that he presents a rather broad view of the topic of cultural unity in Africa and draws conclusions which are difficult to maintain, such as Diop's argument that matrilineal clan systems in Africa were created by men. I think a more practical approach to understanding the cultural unity of Africa is one which is closer to Faraar's approach of looking at Africa's cultural unity as being the result of interaction among different ethnic groups, rather than a cultural unity in Africa which emerged from a singular source. My main point, however, is that respect for women was found throughout Africa and did form the basis for cultural commonalities, which can be viewed as a form of cultural unity.

I want readers to understand that in the United States of America, African people have never been treated equally. We have never been treated as citizens. If this were truly the case, why was Colin Kaepernick kneeling in protest against police brutality? There has never been anything moral or Christian about the United States where African people are concerned, and the fact that this is even a controversial statement to some further proves my point. Historically we have never even been free to truly express how we feel about our struggles, which is why Kaepernick has been receiving so much criticism for daring to express his opinions.

African Americans are made to feel ashamed or guilty about expressing frustrations or anger about the pain and suffering that we have experienced in the United States, and this too can have a detrimental impact on the well-being of the black family because it is emotionally unhealthy for an individual—or a people—to repress such strong negative feelings. In closing, I will say that it is very important that we not allow society to make us feel ashamed or guilty about having these very human responses to hardships and injustices.

8 THE WEAPON OF THEORY: A REFLECTION ON AMILCAR CABRAL

This is a short essay on Amilcar Cabral's theories of anti-colonial struggle.

Amilcar Cabral was one of the founders and the leader of the African Party for the Independence of Guinea and Cape Verde (PAIGC), which fought to liberate Guinea-Bissau and Cape Verde from Portuguese rule. More so than being a revolutionary leader, Cabral was also an agronomist whose vision included national development centered around agriculture. Cabral's struggle and his ideas resonated with Pan-Africanists around the world, including those in the United States and the Caribbean. This can be demonstrated by the fact that Stokely Carmichael (later known as Kwame Ture) had offered to send thirty trained African Americans to join the PAIGC's struggle.

The struggle for independence which Cabral was engaged in was a very brutal one. The Portuguese resorted to torture and massacre, including a massacre in 1959, which killed fifty Africans. Despite this, Cabral still sought to negotiate a peaceful end to the conflict. Carlos Schwarz quoted Cabral as stating that "both sides speak Portuguese and could understand each other each quickly". Cabral also worked to win over the Portuguese soldiers against whom his people fought. In a message to the Portuguese colonial army, Cabral asserted that his people were "not the enemy of the Portuguese people." He continued to explain: "You are the sons of the Portuguese people, but you are being used by the colonialists as tools to kill our people, in order to try to prevent us being free and masters of our own land."

Cabral clarified that the struggle was a struggle against the capitalist ruling class in Portugal, which oppressed Africans in the colonies, and which oppressed the Portuguese people. Cabral explained that this ruling class "exploits the people of Portugal as much as it exploits us." Cabral also explained that the enemy which confronted Africans was not the Portuguese people or Portugal itself, but Portuguese colonialism represented by the fascist government of Portugal.

Cabral noted that Africans answered the Portuguese attempt to bring religion and civilization "with weapons in hands", so there is no mistaking the fact that Cabral was prepared to engage in a serious armed struggle against Portugal for the liberation of his people, but given his Marxist views, Cabral was clearly articulating that he was fighting against a particular class of Portuguese society and not against all Portuguese people.

There may have been a hint of the "double consciousness" which W.E.B. Du Bois wrote about in Cabral's ideology as well. Cabral studied in Portugal. There he met and married his first wife, a Portuguese woman named Maria Helena, with whom Cabral would have two children. Cabral's second wife, Ana Maria, recalled that Cabral's relationship with his wife was not very good. Ana Maria began her relationship with Cabral shortly after Cabral separated from his first wife. I would imagine—and I use the term imagine because I do not know why Cabral's first marriage ended—that there was a significant cultural and political difference between Cabral and his first wife, which perhaps grew as Cabral waged his struggle against Portuguese colonialism. Maria Helena was a Portuguese woman who had moved to Guinea-Bissau with Cabral. Whereas Cabral was an African who was returning back home to liberate his people, Maria Helena was going to Guinea-Bissau as a white settler.

Cabral analogized Portuguese colonialism and the Portuguese settlers to a cart and its wheels. A cart cannot run without wheels. He saw the settlers as being the wheels and colonialism as being the cart. In other words, it was the Portuguese settlers who helped to uphold the colonial domination of Africans in the colonies.

Cabral explained to these settlers: "The colour of your skin has been and goes on being sufficient reason to ensure your supremacy in our lands, in contempt of the feelings, rights, culture, civilization, and just aspirations of our peoples."

Perhaps Cabral saw his marriage to a Portuguese woman as an act of defiance against the racism of the white settlers. He had complained that there were only 60,000 "coloureds" in Angola and Mozambique, and that nearly all of the coloureds were "illegitimate children who have been abandoned by European fathers." Cabral also noted that a mixed couple "especially an African man and European woman, is always a target for the insults and mockery of the settlers, so much so that the very few existing couples do not usually show themselves in public." Here Cabral may have been discussing some of his own experiences when he was married to his first wife.

Within the Portuguese colonial context, Cabral was an assimilated African and he had attempted to use his position to negotiate a peaceful transition to independence with Portugal, but there could be no such peaceful transition from a nation which had enslaved, murdered, raped, and tortured Africans for centuries. Independence could only be obtained through bloodshed, yet until the very end Cabral maintained confidence in a possible peaceful solution, and he continued to urge the Portuguese people to assist in the struggle of Guinea-Bissau.

Cabral was influenced by Marxism. As such, he saw the Portuguese as being an oppressed people just as Africans were oppressed. The two situations were not the same, however. Guinea-Bissau was dominated by a foreign power, which imposed a cultural form of imperialism on the African masses. This is to say that the Portuguese imposed their culture and their way of life on the African masses. Cabral recognized this cultural aspect of European colonialism. He explained that Africans were "crushed by the technical superiority of the imperialist conqueror, with the complicity of or betrayal by some indigenous ruling classes. The elites who were faithful to the history and to the culture of the people were destroyed." Cabral affirmed the achievements of African culture and spoke of the importance of Africa's "cultural resistance" against the dominant colonial powers. Cabral's experiences made him an "assimilado," but he was not content with this. He denounced Portugal's multi-racialism as a myth. Cabral further explained that the people of Guinea-Bissau were struggling for national independence, not struggling to be Portuguese.

Despite rejecting assimilation into the colonial system and affirming the great achievements of Africa's culture, Cabral rejected the notion that there were "racial cultures." Cabral also seemed to have little interest in appeals for racial unity which were not rooted in a common revolutionary struggle. For example, Cabral not only affirmed his support for the liberation struggles in Angola, Mozambique, and other African nations, but he also urged his people to show solidarity with the "descendants of African slaves who are today part of the North American population and are Americans." Cabral also extended this solidarity to the people of Asia, Latin America, and socialist nations in Europe as well. Within this context, Cabral's appeal for solidarity with African Americans was not necessarily an appeal to a common racial identity or an appeal for racial unity. In fact, Cabral pointed out that the people of Guinea-Bissau "have as allies the working class movements in various countries in Europe, or in America, or in Asia—in the capitalist countries of Asia—but above all in Europe and America." For this reason, Cabral urged that his people "develop our ties of friendship and solidarity with these movements."

Cabral especially enjoyed the support of President Sékou Touré of the Republic of Guinea. The headquarters of the PAIGC was located in the Republic of Guinea. Touré's support for the PAIGC made him a target of Portuguese imperialists, which included an attack on Touré's residence which was intended to assassinate him. This failed attempt to kill Touré and destroy the government of Guinea was, according to Cabral, more proof that the Portuguese colonialists "are veritable gangsters or bandits without the slightest scruple, able to commit the most savage crime and to put forward the most shameless lies."

Guinea is also where Kwame Nkrumah went to live after Nkrumah was overthrown in Ghana. In Guinea, Nkrumah was made co-president along with Touré. Following Nkrumah's death, Cabral would praise Nkrumah as "the strategist of genius in the struggle against classic colonialism." Cabral denounced those in

Ghana who betrayed Nkrumah and rejected the "slanderous criticisms" against Nkrumah which "purport to show Nkrumah's economic bankruptcy." Cabral continues: "Everyone knows very well that from 1970, on the basis of all the economic measures taken by Nkrumah and his government, Ghana was to become a fully developing country which would show the world that Africa was not only able to win political independence but also to build its economic independence."

Cabral can perhaps be faulted for downplaying the extent of Ghana's economic problems during Nkrumah's presidency, but there is no denying the fact that Nkrumah was a revolutionary and anti-colonial thinker and Pan-Africanist who was indeed a victim of the "cancer of betrayal" which Cabral spoke of. In Cabral's view, this act of treason against Nkrumah did have one positive aspect. That aspect is that it allowed one to better grasp Nkrumah's true stature as a political giant.

Cabral preached the doctrine of revolutionary democracy. According to Cabral, this meant that "responsible workers and leaders should live among the people, before the people, behind the people. They must work for the Party in the certainty that they are working for the people in our land. And we must struggle so that at all costs the people feel that it is they who have the power in our land in their hands." Cabral also declared that the PAIGC rejected opportunism. In fact, he declared that revolutionary democracy must work to combat opportunism.

Once in power, however, the PAIGC fell short of Cabral's vision of revolutionary democracy. Cabral's half-brother Luis became the first president of Guinea-Bissau until he was overthrown in a military coup in 1980. Amilcar Cabral was certainly aware of these dangers. He began developing the creation of governmental ministries to help keep leaders close to the citizens. He felt that the leaders should work among the people. This of course continues to be a significant problem in post-colonial Africa today.

It is within the post-colonial context that I will conclude this reflection of Cabral's ideas. Cabral's struggle was a struggle against Portuguese colonialism. He did not get the chance to govern the newly independent Guinea-Bissau. He did not even live to see independence. One is certain that the situation in Guinea-

Bissau following independence is not a situation which Cabral himself would have approved of, yet one is also tempted to ask what could Cabral have done differently? What would he have done differently?

Not too long ago I had an exchange with a colleague of mine on the topic of Marxism-Leninism in Africa. That exchange focused mainly on Marxism-Leninism in Angola and Mozambique, which were two former Portuguese colonies which also waged armed struggles for liberation. In that exchange, I particularly noted the challenges that Mozambique experienced. Despite dealing with a civil war and debt, the government of Mozambique remained in power. Yet the government of Guinea-Bissau was overthrown in a carefully organized coup d'état which took place at a time when many of the leading members of the government were outside of the country. This coup took place at a time when there were shortages of rice, as well as other essential provisions.

Despite the political setbacks in Mozambique, the government there maintained the reputation of being one which implemented measures against corruption. In Guinea-Bissau, however, there were allegations of corruption leveled against Luis Cabral and other bureaucrats in the government, who were known for driving expensive cars. There were reports of demonstrations in the streets to celebrate the overthrow of the government.

Portugal was not willing to peacefully grant independence to its colonies as other colonial powers had done, so Guinea-Bissau required an armed struggle to liberate itself. This was not the path which Cabral wished to pursue, however. He wanted a peaceful end to colonialism. His second wife Maria Cabral stated that "Cabral was forced to live with weapons", and that he was always disturbed whenever someone died. It was necessary to build an organized armed force to combat Portuguese colonialism, yet the military has been a source of much of Guinea-Bissau's struggles since independence.

The other reality is that of neo-colonialism. The racism and exploitation of colonialism did not end, though African nations were granted political independence. Several African leaders who led their nations into independence also made the error of leading their nations right into neo-colonialism. This was sometimes done by those who still remained psychologically and emotionally attached to the former colonizer; other times this was done unintentionally by leaders whose policies failed to develop truly self-reliant and independent nations. How would Cabral have navigated through neo-colonialism? Would he have been overthrown as Kwame Nkrumah was or assassinated as Patrice Lumumba and Thomas Sankara had been? We cannot be sure because Cabral's assassination came prior to the ultimate victory of the PAIGC's anti-colonial struggle. What we can be sure of is that Cabral was not merely just an anti-colonial revolutionary who was waging an armed struggle for independence. He was also a Pan-African theorist who was seriously wrestling with questions such as cultural resistance and national development within the context of the anti-colonial struggle.

References:

Amilcar Cabral, *Unity and Struggle: Speeches and Writings*, (Monthly Review Press, 1979).

"Amílcar Cabral: Dedicação e espírito de sacrifício (por Ana Maria Cabral)," *Nos Genti*, September 30, 2012.

Barbara Harrell-Bond and Sarah Forer, "Guinea-Bissau Part 1: The Colonial Experience," *American Universities Field Staff Reports*, 1981.

Carlos Schwarz, "Amilcar Cabral: An Agronomist Before His Time," 2012.

Quito Swan, "Caveat of an Obnoxious Slave: Blueprint for Decolonizing Black Power Studies From the Intellectual Governors of White Supremacy," *The Journal of Pan African Studies*, vol.6, no.2, July 2013.

www.ingramcontent.com/pod-product-compliance
Lightning Source LLC
Chambersburg PA
CBHW071210280526
45787CB00002B/637